LIBRARIES PARTNERING
WITH SELF-PUBLISHING

LIBRARIES PARTNERING WITH SELF-PUBLISHING

A Winning Combination

Robert J. Grover, Kelly Visnak, Carmaine Ternes, Miranda Ericsson, and Lissa Staley

Fountaindale Public Library
Bolingbrook, IL
(630) 759-2102

LIBRARIES
UNLIMITED ™
An Imprint of ABC-CLIO, LLC
Santa Barbara, California • Denver, Colorado

Library of Congress Cataloging-in-Publication Data

Names: Grover, Robert, 1942- author. | Visnak, Kelly, author. | Ternes, Carmaine, author. | Ericsson, Miranda, author. | Staley, Lissa, author.
Title: Libraries partnering with self-publishing : a winning combination / Robert J. Grover, Kelly Visnak, Carmaine Ternes, Miranda Ericsson and Lissa Staley.
Description: Santa Barbara, CA : Libraries Unlimited, [2016] | Includes bibliographical references and index.
Identifiers: LCCN 2016013187 (print) | LCCN 2016032582 (ebook) | ISBN 9781440841583 (paperback) | ISBN 9781440841590 (eBook)
Subjects: LCSH: Libraries and publishing—United States. | Self-publishing—United States. | Electronic publishing—United States. | Libraries and community—United States. | Libraries—Cultural programs—Kansas—Case studies.
Classification: LCC Z716.6 .G76 2016 (print) | LCC Z716.6 (ebook) | DDC 070.5/94--dc23
LC record available at https://lccn.loc.gov/2016013187

ISBN: 978-1-4408-4158-3
EISBN: 978-1-4408-4159-0

20 19 18 17 16   1 2 3 4 5

This book is also available as an eBook.

Libraries Unlimited
An Imprint of ABC-CLIO, LLC

ABC-CLIO, LLC
130 Cremona Drive, P.O. Box 1911
Santa Barbara, California 93116-1911
www.abc-clio.com

This book is printed on acid-free paper ∞
Manufactured in the United States of America

CONTENTS

Contents vii

ACKNOWLEDGMENTS

We are grateful to our many professional colleagues—librarians and writers—who have contributed to this book. We thank our Emporia authors who willingly shared their self-publishing experiences—Tracy Million Simmons, Scott Irwin, and Glen Strickland.

We appreciate the Topeka writing community for expecting more from their library and inspiring the projects and programs we have created together. We thank the authors interviewed here who gave us the words to educate and motivate other self-published writers.

We thank our family members for their support as we spent many hours away from them writing, rewriting, editing, and meeting with our co-authors.

And we thank our acquisitions editor, Blanche Woolls, who encouraged us to write this book and provided guidance along the way.

INTRODUCTION

CHAPTER OVERVIEW

Our world is rapidly changing, and publishing also is experiencing cataclysmic change, providing the opportunity for librarians and writers to engage in a creative and productive partnership. This book is devoted to the evolution of traditional publishing and library service, and the challenges associated with writing and publishing in a digital age. Technology advances have spawned the Open Access movement and have prompted a revolution in publishing and the role of libraries in their support of writers as they conduct research, write, edit, design, and publish their work.

Our world has changed substantially with the invention and widespread use of the computer and Internet. This chapter examines the publishing process within the "life of information" and how it has changed. In addition to introducing the purpose and intended audience, we also outline the contents of the book.

PUBLISHING IS CHANGING

The twenty-first century is fast-paced and characterized by rapid and continuous change. Nearly every aspect of our lives has changed in the last three decades—our values, family structure, education system, communication patterns—in general, the way we live. We live in a much different world than our parents. Some adults find this society challenging and confusing, and they long for a simpler life.

Change is a constant in our world of the twenty-first century, and technological advances fuel that change. Recent advancements in technology have provided new methods for publishing—the way we record and disseminate information. For example, Snapchat combines visual and textual information as well as highlights and layers information for easier comprehension by focusing simultaneously on the sender and receiver of the message. Unlike a book, which appears flat and is designed so that the reader progresses in a linear fashion,

Snapchat and other new social media illustrate nonlinearity and the dynamic interaction of information in various formats, enhanced by bright colors and freestyle design.

Technology enables us to break through the barriers of distance and time to work together solving problems and to learn, as we never have before. The Internet enables instant transmission of information in a variety of formats to numerous sites and people. Electronic books, blogs, Facebook, Twitter, and other social media are forms of communication that result from the technology revolution.

We submit that the driving force for this change in our world is technology, and in this book we explore one important aspect of this change—the publishing process. Indeed, communication and information technologies have changed dramatically the way we create new information and knowledge, how we record it, mass produce it, communicate it, learn from it, use it, and store it.

At the heart of current society in the United States and worldwide is information and knowledge. We can say with assurance that we live in a "knowledge society"; knowledge is essential to our economic system, government, educational system, and even our entertainment. Information is to our society what blood is to our bodies; as our vascular system carries blood to all parts of our bodies, so information and knowledge support virtually all elements of our society.

WHY THIS BOOK IS NEEDED

Technology has changed our lives and the way we communicate; consequently, librarians and other information professionals must take advantage of newer technologies and help their clientele do the same. This book defines "publishing" as the creation, recording, and dissemination of information. In the past, patrons came to the library asking how to get their children's book or their great American novel published. The recording and dissemination processes have been changed by technology and have expanded the capabilities of library and information professionals to help their clientele self-publish books. Needed is a "go to" source for librarians to consult and provide for clientele wanting to publish their books; this book fulfills that need.

PURPOSE OF THIS BOOK

This book provides advice and suggested resources for librarians assisting the large number of clientele who wish to self-publish in various formats. This book serves as a guide to help librarians and their clientele in all types of libraries to understand and participate in the book publishing process, using new technologies and media. It is both a handbook and a guide to other resources to assist the librarian and author in a self-publishing partnership.

AUDIENCE

This book is intended for library and information professionals in schools, public libraries, college and university libraries, and special libraries (government, medical, law, historical, corporate, and government) who may have a general knowledge of technology applications to electronic publishing hardware and software. The book is a guide for both librarians and authors who want to know how to write, design, publish, and market their own books. In other words, this book helps authors and librarians to partner in the book-publishing process.

BOOK OVERVIEW

Chapter 2 is devoted to the changes that have occurred in publishing since we entered the digital age. We describe how computers, word processing, laser printers, and sophisticated copy machines have changed how we think about publishing. Because of these advances in technology, information consumers have become information producers.

Chapter 3 explores "the life of information"—how information is created and communicated to an audience. This chapter outlines the thought processes involved in identifying an audience for a book, assessing their needs for information, and planning a book for self-publishing.

Chapter 4 explores the challenging processes associated with writing and publishing a book. This chapter describes the traditional processes involved in publishing a book commercially so that the reader has a realistic understanding of the time, effort, and hard work that must be invested in self-publishing a book.

Chapter 5 investigates the publishing alternatives, including vanity presses, print-on-demand, and printing options. Distributing and marketing are described and an example is provided of a self-published book from concept to marketing.

Chapter 6 describes, with examples, activities that libraries can sponsor to assist clientele who are writers or artists who want to publish their own works.

Chapter 7 is a description of the successful writers' program developed by the Topeka and Shawnee County (Kansas) Public Library. Two authors of this book share their experiences working with writers and provide useful information for both librarians and writers.

Chapter 8 discusses social media that can be used to promote or market a book. Included are Facebook, YouTube, Twitter, Instagram, Tumblr, Flickr, and Pinterest with examples of libraries that are effectively using social media to promote reading and services.

Chapter 9 describes how the Open Access movement brings libraries and information professionals into research and publishing. The Open Access movement has encouraged rethinking and restructuring of the research and publishing processes. Academic libraries have provided leadership in this movement, with opportunities for collaboration with other types of libraries.

Chapter 10 is a bibliographic essay listing books, Web sites, and Internet sources on such how-to topics as creating a Web site and designing, printing, and marketing a book. It is intended for librarians and library clientele wanting to "do their own thing."

DEFINING TERMS

Before going further, we will clarify our terms used in discussing the publishing process.

Information

In a previous work (Greer, Grover, and Fowler 2013), we defined "data," "information," and "knowledge," using definitions by Harland Cleveland in his book *The Knowledge Executive* (1985).

"Data are the rough materials from which information and knowledge are formed, i.e., undigested observations, or unvarnished facts, as Cleveland calls them" (Greer, Grover, and Fowler 2013, 9).

Information is organized data, which is given context. For example, the number 25 is meaningless unless we provide the context of an outdoor temperature in degrees on a February day. A temperature of 25 degrees Fahrenheit is information.

Knowledge

Knowledge is organized information that is integrated into an individual's knowledge system. Knowledge has been evaluated by the individual and accepted as "truth." When we read the news in a newspaper or on our tablet computer or watch the television news, we remember only a small portion of that information. What we remember becomes personal knowledge. We have selected information, processed it, and synthesized it to become knowledge.

In a similar way, knowledge is selected and processed by groups of people—what we refer to as "social knowledge" when we discuss the life cycle of information. Social knowledge, like personal knowledge, is subjected to analysis, selection, and synthesis before acceptance by a group or society.

To better understand how publishing fits into the life cycle of information and knowledge, we'll now explore the concept of "information transfer."

Information Transfer

A key concept for understanding the publishing process is "information transfer," a way of thinking about the life cycle of information. In another work we defined information transfer as "the communication of a recorded message from one human or human mind to another" (Greer, Grover, and Fowler 2013, 59). We make a distinction between communication and information transfer in this way: the sender and receiver of communication usually are contemporaries; however, information transfer requires a recorded message. Consequently, the sender and receiver may not be contemporaries.

Information has a "life"; the stages in the life of information are the following:

- Creation
- Recording
- Reproduction
- Dissemination
- Organization of information
- Diffusion
- Utilization
- Preservation
- Discarding

This model is important for understanding the entire publishing process. Each of these stages of the information transfer cycle is described briefly below and based on our earlier work.

Creation

Information is created by the assembly of data in ways that provide new meanings or understandings that show new relationships. For example, researchers may conduct a formal study of the way that a group of people uses information. Another example is the coverage of a news event by a reporter for a local newspaper, television, or radio station. A third example is an individual who posts ideas on a Web page, blog, or Facebook entry, perhaps assembling ideas from several sources and synthesizing them into a post. Newer technologies enable an individual to create, record, and make information available for a public quickly through the use of these technologies.

In these examples, new information was created. Data and observations were assembled into new information. Authors begin a work with this process; creation is only the first step in the information transfer process, and the information has little meaning until it is synthesized and recorded.

Recording

After a body of information is created, it must be recorded in some format so that it can be disseminated and used by others. In the case of formal research, researchers collect data, and the data are analyzed to reveal trends. The analysis of data is synthesized into a report of the research process and the findings. This preparation of a report is the recording stage.

In the example of a news event, the reporter must then assemble her notes into a report of the event. In the third example, the creator synthesized information for recording on a Web site, blog, or Facebook posting. Unlike the other two examples, there was no editor to serve as a filter for the information before the author recorded her thoughts. The creator served both roles.

In all three examples, data that were collected were synthesized and recorded. The recording may be accomplished digitally, using a word processor. If reporters were working for a television station, their reports might be recorded digitally and posted on the station's Web site after they reported live during the local 6:00 p.m. televised news program. Regardless of format, the new information has been recorded as the second stage of the information transfer cycle.

The author who self-publishes has a choice of formats for mass producing and disseminating the information. These formats are discussed in later chapters.

Reproduction

This stage is an essential part of publishing as we know it. Reproduction of information requires copying the information so that it can be distributed. Traditional book publishing requires expensive presses and other equipment to print, trim, and collate books. With electronic reproduction and dissemination, the mass production may be instantaneous with the dissemination. In the example of formal research, researchers send their finished report of the research project to a journal that is likely to publish a report on the topic. At this point an evaluation process occurs. A scholarly journal editor will scan the manuscript and select a group of peers to review the report.

A newspaper or other mass media outlet has in place a similar review process before a story is published, aired, or placed on a Web page. An editor reviews the reporter's work, and with the concurrence of the managing editor assigns the story to a place in the newspaper so that it can be mass-produced. A television news reporter, like a newspaper reporter, covers stories assigned by an editor. Similarly, a news director selects stories that are aired. Most newspapers, radio, and television news outlets now post stories and supplementary information on their Web sites, blogs, and perhaps on social media like Twitter.

In the example of individuals who assemble information and post an entry on a Web site, blog, or on social media, the mere posting of the information results in "mass production" of the information. The posting can be done quickly from one's home computer or while traveling and using a laptop, tablet computer, or smartphone.

Scholarly and popular news media and publishing houses have in place an editing process. A person (or several people) with experience and expertise in reporting or in research reviews the work of a news reporter or the writing of a scholar. However, technological advances have reduced the cost of mass production so that desktop publishing and Internet publishing enable individuals to mass-produce and disseminate information without benefit of the screening that has been a common feature in the past. Self-publishing is now more feasible than before we had access to the Internet.

When a work is self-published, the author may be the editor as well, although it's always better to have "other eyes" read the document for accuracy, clarity, and grammatical construction. We'll discuss this aspect of self-publishing in a later chapter.

Dissemination

After information has been mass-produced, it can be distributed to an audience—another important stage in self-publishing. Technology has created new ways to disseminate information more quickly and more cheaply than ever before.

Traditionally, dissemination has required a publisher to print and market books as part of the dissemination process. The publisher sends review copies to publications likely to review the book for their audience, issues catalogs, and advertises the new publication in appropriate journals or other media. The publisher takes orders for the books, sends them to buyers, and may also send copies to a book jobber who will store copies and accept orders. Marketing the book is a major part of the dissemination process.

Through the application of technology, individuals now have the ability to create, record, mass-produce, and disseminate information without the intrusion of an editor or censor. The author or creator has immediate access to a wide audience through the Internet and through print-on-demand services. Marketing and selling is also a responsibility of the self-published author. The various means of dissemination or distribution are discussed further in Chapter 5.

Organization of Information

Throughout the history of the library profession, bibliography has been central to the profession. The result of this professional focus has been the creation of national libraries, the copyright law, national bibliographies, library catalogs, indexes, and subject bibliographies.

Organization of information through such tools as bibliographies, indexes, and catalogs is essential for the efficient retrieval and use of information, and the library profession has taken a general approach to organizing information. Terms used for subject headings are standardized but are not necessarily the terms used by the library's clientele. Limits were placed on the number of subject headings that could be used for card catalogs of library collections; however, advancements in computer technology have enabled the use of key words in addition to subject headings or descriptors in searching for and retrieving information. The use of such search engines as Google and others provides additional retrieval capability, including full-text searching of manuscripts.

The author of a self-published book must consider the organization of the book as identified in the table of contents, which acts as a guide to the content. Another important organizational device is a nonfiction book's index, which enables readers to identify certain ideas, people, or subjects. An index requires specialized knowledge, as suggested in Chapter 4.

Individuals who post on a Web site or blog might have their information accessed by a user who uses a search engine. Thanks to advances in technology, the organization and retrieval of information have been enhanced with the sophistication of computer technology.

Diffusion

After information is disseminated and organized, it is the mission of librarians and other professionals to diffuse the information, that is, to help information users to understand this information and to make sense of it—to help people learn the information so that they can put it to use.

It has traditionally been the task of librarians to acquire, organize, store, and disseminate information for their public. Because technology has transformed the information transfer process, it is important for librarians and other information professionals to become more engaged in the diffusion of information as well as dissemination. This book presumes that librarians are also involved in diffusing—or teaching—those authors wanting to self-publish.

How do diffusion and dissemination differ? Dissemination refers to making information available, as a book makes information available to the public. Diffusion is assisting in the understanding of information, as a teacher or librarian interprets a novel to help a reader understand the characters, theme, and setting. History books disseminate information about historical events of humankind; history teachers help students understand those historical events—teachers facilitate diffusion of history.

Technology has changed diffusion of information and knowledge. Schools and institutions of higher learning are using technology as learning tools in the classroom, and technology is used to reach distant students. Teachers in elementary schools can take students on "field trips" to other countries via the Internet; a Spanish class in Illinois can partner with a class in Peru. Schools and universities are no longer place-bound; their reach has been extended beyond the campus to the country and world beyond. Librarians and authors must be aware of newer teaching and learning technologies that can be used in the author/librarian partnership.

Utilization

Professions of all types are charged with facilitating the use of information. Each profession has a body of specialized knowledge that has application in society. Physicians acquire knowledge of the human body, diseases, treatments, and medicine, and apply that knowledge for the treatment of their patients. Similarly, librarians and other information professionals apply knowledge about the information transfer processes to facilitate the use of knowledge in society.

The previous section on diffusion is required before utilization. Information must be diffused through libraries, schools, organizations, and professions so that individuals and groups can understand information—give it meaning—prior to utilization.

This book is intended to help librarians help authors who want to self-publish their books. In other words, this book will help both librarians and authors to utilize knowledge about publishing as they work together to publish an authored work.

Preservation

Preservation is the retention of recorded information for future availability and use. Preservation includes maintenance of the physical information package (book, journal, etc.) or artifact as well as the ideas recorded in them.

For example, a book may be valued as a physical object because a particular printer or publisher published it, or it may be a first edition of a celebrated author. Or an item may be preserved because of the content—the author's thinking or ideas have value today although written many years ago. The ideas are worthy of study today.

Advances in technology have transformed preservation. Preservation of social media, Web sites, and blogs is complicated for organizations of all sizes. Which parts of a corporate Web site should be preserved? Should e-mail be preserved and for what period of time? Organizations should develop policies for the preservation of information in keeping with their mission.

Discarding

In a library, records may be discarded and destroyed if the content is obsolete, or if the physical condition of the object is beyond repair. Resources in a collection must be evaluated regularly, just as services must be evaluated. Resources should be discarded when they no longer contribute to the mission of the organization. Likewise, authors must be mindful of the accuracy and currency of information included in a publication. Outdated information must be discarded and updated. Librarians can be very helpful in this process.

The information transfer cycle represents the life cycle for information in any format. It is helpful to consider this model when thinking about publishing and the role of librarians, information professionals, and authors in the publishing process. Individuals considering self-publication will find the model helpful for understanding the many aspects of publication beyond the writing process. The information transfer model adapts to accommodate new technologies as they arise; although some of the stages of information transfer have been merged by technology, the model is adaptable.

For a more comprehensive explanation of the information transfer process, see Greer, Grover, and Fowler (2013, 59–69).

CHAPTER SUMMARY

We define "publishing" as the creation, recording, and dissemination of information—processes that have changed substantially because of advances in technology. Publishing a book is now easier for individuals to accomplish. Librarians should be knowledgeable about the publishing processes and resources available to help their clientele self-publish.

This book provides advice and suggested resources for librarians assisting the growing number of clientele who wish to self-publish; it serves as a guide to help librarians and library clientele in libraries of all types. It is both a handbook and a guide to other resources to assist the librarian and author in a self-publishing partnership.

REFERENCES

Cleveland, Harlan. 1985. *The Knowledge Executive; Leadership in an Information Society.* New York: Truman Talley Books/E. P. Dutton.

Greer, Roger C., Robert J. Grover, and Susan G. Fowler. 2013. *Introduction to the Library and Information Professions.* 2nd ed. Santa Barbara, CA: Libraries Unlimited.

2
___

HOW PUBLISHING HAS CHANGED

CHAPTER OVERVIEW

The computer, word processing, laser printers, and sophisticated printing technology have changed how we think about publishing. This chapter examines publishing as it has been in years past before the current state of book publishing described in Chapter 3. We begin with a brief look back in time at communication and the social changes that have influenced the way we record and disseminate information.

EVOLUTION OF PUBLISHING

Information transfer (defined in Chapter 1) in general and publishing in particular have been central to the evolution of human society. Expression of ideas through recorded messages has evolved from the time of the cave dwellers to the present. Here we sketch briefly the evolution of publishing as a background for discussion of our current publishing milieu. The brief history that follows is based on a recent work by the authors (Grover et al. 2015).

Early Recorded Messages

Information transfer by definition is the exchange of recorded information; therefore, it is helpful to explore briefly how communication and recorded messages have changed over time. Meadow (2006, 1) provides a standard definition of communication: "Communication is based on the transmission of symbols and the interpretation of these symbols by the receiver of the communication." Symbols may be sounds, including spoken words; pictures; digital symbols (letters, numbers); odors; tastes; and touch. In other words, humans communicate using all of their senses.

Drawings thought to be 50,000 years old have been discovered in caves in France and Spain. These drawings were iconic—pictures of objects or animals. About 3300 BCE the Sumerians recorded symbols on the flat surface of clay tablets. Pictorial symbols gradually evolved into abstract symbols representing subjects and ideas. The English alphabet was created by Semitic peoples who lived in the region of present-day Lebanon, Israel, Palestine, and Egypt.

"Publishing" from ancient times through the Middle Ages was essentially handwriting on clay tablets, then on scrolls, and later in the codex form of recording—the book format of bound pages as we know it. The codex format originated during the Roman Empire and was much easier to use and more compact than scrolls. Although the format was an improvement, hand copying of books was labor intensive and time consuming.

The material on which symbols were recorded evolved from papyrus, parchment made from sheepskin, and vellum made from calfskin. Ink was used as early as 2500 BCE. Paper was invented in China about 100 CE (Meadow 2006).

The Renaissance in the fourteenth century and the Reformation of the sixteenth century resulted in more people reading and writing. These efforts to read were supported by the invention of the printing press in 1454 by Johannes Gutenberg, who combined advancements in metalwork, paper presses, and engineering to develop a printing press with movable type. Gutenberg improved the printing process by refining both typesetting and the printing processes. The printing press enabled the fast reproduction of newspapers, magazines, pamphlets, and books.

Other economic factors were the capability of printing on both sides of a page in the codex format and the development of thinner paper to replace parchment. The availability of paper and the improved process of printing revolutionized the reproduction, mass production, and dissemination of information at a time when a growing middle class needed education and materials to enable widespread teaching and learning.

The invention of mechanical movable-type printing led to a large increase in printing activities across Europe. Printing spread to cities throughout Europe by the end of the fifteenth century. European printing presses in 1600 were capable of producing 3,600 impressions per day, compared to movable-type printing in Asia, where printing was done by manually rubbing the back of the paper to the typeset page, which would produce 40 pages per day. The improvement of publishing potential resulted in faster dissemination of ideas. More than 750,000 copies of Erasmus's works were distributed during his lifetime, and Martin Luther's works were distributed in 300,000 printed copies. The ideas of Erasmus and Luther have transcended time because they were recorded, mass-produced, and distributed because of advances in technology.

Photography

Photography, recording visual images on a surface such as a sheet of paper, was popularized with Frenchman Louis Daguerre's invention of the daguerreotype in 1829. This method used copper plates coated with silver iodide, but ten years later in England Frederick Archer used glass plates covered with different chemicals, a more practical process.

In 1889 Thomas Edison invented a way of projecting photographs of a moving subject, resulting in the illusion that the images were moving—the origin of movies. In 1888 George Eastman began using paper coated with emulsion to make photographs, replacing the bulky glass plates previously used, and Eastman Kodak Company was formed. Photography soon became a means of recording family events and news events, and with the development of motion pictures, photography became the best way of communicating visual information until the invention of television.

The Internet

Computers alone cannot transmit information; however, computers have enabled establishment of the worldwide communication network we know as the Internet. The U.S. Department of Defense initially sponsored computer science research for a communication system that linked computers. The Advanced Research Projects Agency (ARPA) conducted the research that developed a network of computers called ARPANET in 1969. The network linked computers via telephone lines at research facilities in the United States and enabled the transfer of files among computers—communication that became known as e-mail.

ARPANET was expanded beyond government agencies to private companies, and in 1983 an international set of standards (Internet) was implemented. That term became used to describe the worldwide network. Key components are the Internet Service Providers (ISPs), which provide access for individuals to any other computer on the network. While some people may call the Internet "the global information infrastructure," we submit that it is only one component (albeit a very important one) in the information infrastructure.

Communication Satellites

A relatively recent addition to the global information infrastructure is the communication satellite. First proposed in a scientific paper written in 1945, the earliest satellite was launched by the U.S. Air Force in 1958. To be effective, a satellite must be in geosynchronous orbit—move around the earth at the same rate that the earth turns—so that the satellite appears to be stationary. Meadow (2006, 84) describes a communication satellite "like a very tall tower that can receive radio signals and retransmit them." Most satellites are about 22,300 miles above the earth. Communication satellites are now a vital link in the global information infrastructure.

Wireless Telephone

The wireless telephone or cell phone was invented in 1947 as a mobile radio connected to a telephone system. Range for use was very limited, but the first cellular phone system was initiated in 1979 in Tokyo. The U.S. government approved the use of cellular phones in the United States in 1982. Cell phones provide the capability to connect with the Internet, send and receive text messages, download software, receive and send pictures, play recorded music, as well as provide telephone service.

Currently the cell phone has evolved into a multipurpose information receiver, recorder, and disseminator. Most "smartphones" have the capability of taking still photographs and motion pictures. They can send and receive text messages as well as telephone calls. Cell phones can access the Internet and send and receive e-mail. It is now possible for people to communicate with others wherever they are able to receive radio signals and to receive and transmit oral messages, photographs, and motion pictures from a device that fits in one's hand.

A Participatory Culture

The merging of these communication technologies has provided easier access to information consumers. Access to the Internet, enabled by sophisticated networks using satellite transmission, cell phones, and portable computers, has enabled people worldwide to have access to new ways of creating, recording, and disseminating information. As the authors have declared in an earlier work, a participatory culture has evolved:

> The Internet provides an ideal space for a participatory culture by simply providing information freely in an open and widely distributed way. Online stories and video games have moved people into a culture of participation. Readers who unite through the Internet participate in solving a riddle and then gain access to the next chapter in the book; they are involved in a new and collaborative way of using information. (Grover et al. 2015, 4)

Through the capabilities provided by elaborate communication technologies, people throughout the world have access to the Internet via their cell phones. Smartphones combine the telephone with computers, photography, radio, television, and audio/video recordings. Furthermore, through these communication technologies individuals may participate in the creation and dissemination of information; the process is no longer one-way communication to the consumer.

People can use their cell phones as cameras to record events as motion pictures or still photographs and transmit them via e-mail or social media to friends and family across town or across the country. A writer can create a blog or Web site and share her ideas with an audience anywhere in the world. The readership can participate in the conversation with their comments on Facebook, Twitter, or by adding comments to a blog or other social media. In this digital age, ideas can be recorded and disseminated, overcoming the past barriers of distance and time. These technologies have created a new paradigm in book publishing—self-publishing.

TECHNOLOGY ADVANCES HAVE CHANGED PUBLISHING

Publishing includes the processes of writing or recording, copyediting, graphic design, printing, marketing, and distribution. Technology has influenced change in virtually every aspect of society and every process of publishing. Our entertainment has been transformed. Television programming has exploded from three major networks to hundreds of channels that cater to a wide variety of tastes. The Internet enables us to retrieve instantly information on any topic. Newspapers and magazines are available in print and online. Our phone is more than a phone—it's at once a telephone, television, private movie theater, and information source through the World Wide Web.

Just as television and telephones have been transformed by technology, so the publishing industry has been transformed. The major publishing houses still remain the foundations of the book publishing industry, just as the major television networks still are foundations of the television industry. However, publishers have merged in order to survive, and their monopoly on publishing has been shattered by technology. Because of computers and word processing, printers, the Internet, e-mail, and social media, we have a greater opportunity to write and publish our own books. We no longer must go through the long, cumbersome, and frustrating process of "selling" our book to a big publisher. In fact, the self-publishing industry is growing, and we can be a part of it. We can be our own publisher. That's the central message of this book for librarians to share with customers.

Although we may think of this technology revolution as a "new age," the wheels of change have been turning for several decades. As Kasdorf (2003, 2) explains,

Although it may feel as if we're witnessing the birth of a new era, the real revolutions have already happened. The most fundamental is the realization that the published content is independent of the physical products that convey it to us. This was always the case, of course; but it was not until the digital era that we fully appreciated that a book or article is not inextricably bound up in the stacks of paper on which we read it. This is profoundly liberating.

Format has changed, forced by technology advances. Darnton (2009, 23) illustrates the rapid pace of change:

- From writing to codex—4,300 years
- From the codex to movable type—1,150 years
- From movable type to the Internet—524 years
- From the Internet to search engines—17 years
- From search engines to Google's algorithmic relevance ranking—7 years

Google began to revolutionize the way we access books when it signed agreements with five research libraries to digitize their books—Harvard University, Michigan, Stanford, Oxford Bodleian, and New York Public Library. The project was named Google Book Search.

Publishers are making content available on mobile and e-book formats, encouraging readers to make the change to digital formats. Digital formats are advantageous to publishers: "I think we will also see more responsive publishing because, as turnaround times are so much speedier for e-books, publishers producing digital content can respond with speed to consumer trends or crazes—maximizing profitability" (Lossius 2014).

Furthermore, the digital age brings us a wealth of options unavailable to authors in times past. Certainly, a printed work on paper is available to us; nevertheless many more possibilities also are available. A document printed on paper also can be published as a digital book, an e-book, or it can be stored on a Web site for recipients to access. We can limit access by encryption and require payment for that access, or we can lease the document to a commercial publisher, who will publish the document as a paper document or e-book or both.

Still other options are available. Digital technology renders color photographs or illustrations more affordable. Digital format enables the inclusion of audio and video recordings to expand the communication. For example, a book about flower arranging can include a link to a short video recording that illustrates an arrangement. Also, references to other journal articles, Web sites, or even e-books can include links that take the reader directly to a source (as we do in this book).

Digitization also changes the publishing process by expediting communication. Communication time between authors and editors has been dramatically reduced from the days when a paper copy was sent by courier or the postal service. E-mail provides for the instant digital transmission of book proposals, manuscripts, and edited documents for proofreading. Real-time communication via telephone, of course, remains possible, but recorded communication has speeded up exponentially.

Open Access

Digitization has also resulted in the Open Access movement, which has become prominent in colleges and universities. Because the Internet opens dissemination of information to a large population, new models for the publication process have arisen. The Open Access movement provides librarians the opportunity to take leadership by collaborating with university faculty to create teaching resources in order to decrease the textbook cost for students.

In 2008 Congress passed the National Institutes of Health (NIH) Open Access Public Policy, creating a legal mandate that any peer-reviewed article supported by NIH funding could be made freely available to the public via PubMed Central within a year of the publication date. Since passage of the Open Access Public Policy in 2008, national funding bodies have been requiring publicly funded research to be made publicly available. This requirement has been expanded to include data in addition to the published scholarly articles of the findings associated with the grants.

Librarians are closely engaged as liaisons with faculty to facilitate the storage of digital documents and their organization for easy access. Authors can also choose to make their work available to the public through a commercial publisher.

The Open Access movement is not restricted to academic libraries. For example, a similar approach has been launched by the Los Gatos (California) Public Library, which has created a portal on the library Web site that enables authors to post their works (Staley 2015, 19). More information about this type of publishing is found in Chapter 9.

New Formats

Technology has enabled many improvements in the publishing process:

- Thousands of fonts are now widely available.
- Scanning technology enables authors to capture better images.
- Page design software is readily available for desktop publishing.
- Illustrations can be produced and edited easily.
- Management of color in the design and printing process is more reliable.
- Production of print-ready copy has been simplified. (adapted from Kasdorf 2003)

All of these advancements make it possible for aspiring writers in the general public to write and market their own books outside the exclusive control of traditional publishing houses. In the following sections we discuss some of the newer services available to authors who want to publish their own works.

Print-on-Demand

This same technology enables print-on-demand (POD). A digital press makes copies from a digital file and has very little setup cost. Offset printing requires the publisher to run several hundred copies to cover setup costs, often producing an inventory that is not sold. The advantage of POD is that the first copy costs about the same as the 200th copy, and a publisher can print copies as orders come in (printed on demand). Therefore, POD is a way to print copies of a book without investing in an inventory and designating storage space for copies that may not sell.

E-books

Development of the computer was accompanied by development of systems that support computer-based reading but were handicapped by mainframe computers with a limited number of workstations. Development of the personal computer in the 1970s supported the concept of electronic publications that could be read by individuals in the home, office, or school. During the 1990s, hardware, reading systems, and content moved into the marketplace, but e-books were not practical until inexpensive, portable, functional reading devices became available in the early 2000s. Such devices as the Amazon Kindle, Barnes and Noble Nook, and Kobo Aura are popular and highly rated e-book readers. Of course, tablet computers, smartphones, and laptops also suffice as convenient readers for e-books.

Renear and Salo (2003) list the advantages of e-books:

- Capacity—a person can carry scores of books in a lightweight, portable e-book [reader].
- Manufacturing—copying digital files into new storage media can produce e-books inexpensively and quickly.
- Distribution—e-books can be distributed quickly and inexpensively over the Internet.
- Cost—the production cost of electronic books is much less than the cost of printed books.
- Viewing options—reading options can be customized to the reader; the reader can adjust colors, fonts, and font size.
- Navigation—the reader can advance through the document in paragraphs, sections, or problems instead of pages.
- Retrieval—most reading devices permit the retrieval of specific words or phrases, a faster retrieval technique than using an index or table of contents.
- Currency—e-books can be updated frequently and inexpensively, and mistakes can be corrected and information updated.
- Multimedia—e-books can present audio and video content to augment text.
- Accessibility—persons with visual disabilities can easily adjust type size and color to meet their needs.

As more sophisticated reading devices enter the marketplace, consumers who are hesitant to "curl up" with a digital book are tempted to take the leap into the digital age and try e-books. However, it is doubtful that the paperback or hardback book will disappear from the marketplace or from libraries any time soon.

Information Consumers Have Become Information Producers

Publishing has been democratized because of technology, and a participatory culture has emerged, as noted above. With the Internet, blogs, YouTube, and other social media we can "publish" our thoughts within seconds to friends and relatives no matter their location. While a Facebook post is an informal type of publishing, we can use the technology available to us to write, duplicate, distribute, and market books about our hobby, or historical accounts of our community, our family, our service club, or the family business. We can publish a book for a small number of people (our family) or for a larger audience (our town or region). Or we may wish to write and publish our personal memoir and make it available to the general public.

A term applied to publishing for a limited market is "micropublishing." The *Merriam-Webster Dictionary* (2015) defines the term: "publishing in microform." Crawford (2012, 3) provides a more cogent definition: "Micropublishing uses print on demand fulfillment services to publish books that may serve niches from one to 500 copies, by producing books individually as they are needed." Recognizing that every book is not designed to be a bestseller is a relatively new concept that was less likely with traditional publishing.

LIBRARIANS AND AUTHORS: PARTNERS IN PUBLISHING

Librarians can participate in this changing publishing industry, of course, but they can also help clientele who want to publish a book. That's also this book's purpose. As Crawford (2012) suggests, micropublishing books for a niche market will not sell a large number of copies. Self-publishing, or micropublishing, requires a knowledge of the publishing industry and use of new technologies to avoid the economic pitfalls that can lure the uninformed individual. Crawford (2012, 5) states that librarians and libraries should be engaged in self-publishing, "Because it's a great fit with your mission and a new niche that should improve your community standing."

Many libraries provide such services as book discussion groups and offer meeting space and support for hobby clubs, civic organizations, local history groups, family history groups, and local author groups. These groups may have a desire to record and publish their projects, and the library is a likely source of information and support for that activity. Young adults in high school and college may wish to micropublish their collective poetry and short stories. Librarians and libraries have the opportunity to engage actively in the creative process of assisting authors of all ages who wish to make their work available to a larger audience. Friends' groups may also want to take advantage of these opportunities.

Increasingly libraries are reaching wider audiences by providing services that go beyond the expectations of collecting and checking out books. Librarians recognize that in our technological, global society we are increasingly a highly oral and visual society. Consequently, librarians must continuously assess the interests and needs of their communities and modify the mission of their libraries to break the stereotypes and address the ever-changing needs of their communities.

Academic and public libraries are joining museums in providing "makerspaces"—places dedicated to creation, collaboration, and problem solving. Makerspaces may be devoted to do-it-yourself craft projects or to creating science projects. They may provide space and opportunity for engagement in areas that are categorized as science, technology, engineering, art, and mathematics (STEAM) opportunities, where teens meet and learn computer coding. The "maker movement" is all about the library supporting people as they create information packages. Although libraries in the past only collected and disseminated information packages, now libraries of all types are supporting the creation of information packages.

Library and information professionals can create an image for their libraries that announces the library as a place for clientele to engage in thinking, learning, and creating. The programs offered might be topics that enrich the cultural fabric of a community. Libraries of the twenty-first century can create places that feel comfortable for people to create, build, innovate, and collaborate with others in the community.

Furthermore, librarians understand how technology changes each of the information transfer processes. The traditional single author gives way to multiple voices, fast change, and lack of control. The Internet and social media eliminate the ability of individuals and governments to control the exchange of ideas. In the past, new technologies like Gutenberg's printing press facilitated the mass production of information and new knowledge to larger audiences. Now the creation and dissemination of information can circumvent the former gatekeepers—publishers, broadcasters, and media producers—so that individuals with access to public library computers or those with smartphones, tablet computers, or laptops can self-publish books and disseminate them through the Internet and social media. Barriers of time, distance, and cost have been drastically reduced.

The Open Access movement challenges the traditional model for academic publishing, which may not be sustainable with the widespread availability of newer technologies. The objectives of the Open Access movement are to:

- maintain peer review standards of quality for research while making journal articles and other academic publications available free for access and reading;
- publish with some other means of recovering costs—e.g., subsidies or charges for hard copy publications; and
- modify traditional copyright practices so that academic work can be used more freely as a foundation for additional research. ("Berlin Declaration" 2003)

Establishment of a repository accompanies implementation of open access. Librarians must partner with university faculty so that faculties are aware of issues related to storing and organizing research data and the alternatives for disseminating research results. In the traditional research and publication process, a researcher or research team worked independently as they collected, stored, and analyzed data. Often the librarian was consulted only to identify and retrieve information resources needed for research.

With establishment of a repository on campus, the librarian is a valuable member of a research team, providing guidance and assistance in the organization and storage of data in a repository. The librarian can assist in preparing a document for dissemination, clarifying copyright issues, and protecting the researcher's creative work. The librarian also can assist in locating suitable commercial or academic presses for wide dissemination of the work and with self-publishing.

Regardless of the type of institution, the repository can further the university's mission, and it requires change in the way that faculty, librarians, and students use information and fulfill their professional roles. Repositories are not restricted to colleges and universities. A repository is a storehouse for knowledge that's created locally. Librarians can transform the role of repositories to support content curation and to support people developing their own content, whether print, video, or multimedia.

Today anyone can create videos or books, edit or create entries in Wikipedia, create a Web site, or create another kind of information source. Readers or viewers of these information sources also have the opportunity to critique the information online. The information consumer can be a creator as well as critic of information sources.

A trend for all libraries and information agencies is the need to remain relevant to the people they serve and to the people who provide them with funding. Librarians must be engaged with their communities, providing value-added services. Chapter 6 suggests ways that librarians in all types of libraries can partner with authors to self-publish—a value-added service for the digital age.

CHAPTER SUMMARY

Advances in technology have changed how we think about publishing. As communication changed with improvements in technology, information transfer was expedited. Development of computers and telecommunications technologies transcended barriers of time and space, creating a participatory culture in which information consumers also have become information producers. In this digital age, a time of continuous and massive change, librarians have the knowledge and skills to engage with writers who want to self-publish their work. Now is the time to initiate this winning partnership.

REFERENCES

"Berlin Declaration on Open Access to Knowledge in the Sciences and Humanities." 2003. http://openaccess.mpg.de/286432/Berlin-Declaration.

Crawford, Walt. 2012. *The Librarian's Guide to Micropublishing: Helping Patrons and Communities Use Free and Low-Cost Publishing Tools to Tell Their Stories.* Medford, NJ: Information Today.

Darnton, Robert. 2009. *The Case for Books: Past, Present, and Future.* New York: Public Affairs.

Grover, Robert J., Roger C. Greer, Herbert K. Achleitner, and Kelly Visnak. 2015. *The Evolving Information Infrastructure and Information Transfer.* Santa Barbara, CA: Libraries Unlimited.

Kasdorf, William E. 2003. "Introduction: Publishing in Today's Digital Era." In *The Columbia Guide to Digital Publishing*, ed. William E. Kasdorf, 1–31. New York: Columbia University Press.

Lossius, George. 2014. "5 Trends for Trade Publishing in 2014." http://publishingperspectives.com/2014/01/5-trends-for-trade-publishing-in-2014.

Meadow, Charles T. 2006. *Messages, Meaning, and Symbols: The Communication of Information.* Lanham, MD: Scarecrow Press.

Merriam-Webster Dictionary. 2015. "Micropublishing." http://www.merriam-webster.com/dictionary/micropublishing.

Renear, Allen, and Dorothea Salo. 2003. "Electronic Books and the Open eBook Publication Structure." In *The Columbia Guide to Digital Publishing*, ed. William E. Kasdorf, 455–520. New York: Columbia University Press.

Staley, Lissa. 2015. "Leading Self-Publishing Efforts in Communities." *American Libraries* 46: 18–19.

3

PLANNING YOUR BOOK

CHAPTER OVERVIEW

This chapter outlines the thought processes involved in planning a book, whether for self-publishing or for submission to a commercial publisher. In this chapter we begin with the planning that a writer does and the processes associated with commercial book publishing. The stages of book publishing are described and are applicable whether or not a commercial publisher will be sought. A publisher provides valuable expertise in the editing, design, indexing, printing, distribution, and marketing of a book, processes that must be addressed by an author when self-publishing.

Planning early in the process is important. Using the elements of a typical book proposal can serve as an outline for the author to follow. The intended audience is a very important variable, an essential element in the decision-making process.

When the manuscript is complete, the author must make a decision either (1) to acquire an agent, (2) to submit a book proposal to an acquisition editor at a publishing house, or (3) to self-publish.

BEGINNING THE CREATIVE PROCESS

Authoring a book is a creative process. As with painting on canvas, photography, sculpture, music composition, or playwriting, a book begins with an idea that the author wants to communicate. In some cases, as with poetry or some nonfiction works, authors may compile many of their works collected over time. Words are the authors' medium, and they express their thoughts and emotions to create a work that can be read and experienced by another.

How authors proceed is a function of their learning style, their predisposition for thinking and organizing their thoughts. They may take an analytical, thoughtful, step-by-step approach, or they may just "hang loose" and start writing without any consideration for the final product until a later point. How one proceeds is a personal choice; there's no one "correct" way for engaging the creative process.

Unlike some other artists—painters, for example—authors have control over their work only to a point if they publish commercially. The painter selects the topic and the medium, and controls the creative process. In the publishing world, there is a certain amount of negotiation with editors and others engaged in the publishing process. Here we will confine our thinking to the author's role, and the involvement of others in the publishing process will be introduced later.

Audience

It's helpful, even in the early stages of writing, to begin thinking of the intended audience, just as one thinks about communicating with individuals through conversation because writing is a communication process. Based on the age, experience, and our knowledge of the persons in the audience, writers regulate their vocabulary and comments to address the unique characteristics of the individuals they are talking to: a general audience, children, young adults, or a select audience (teachers, retired adults, or a particular profession). The intended audience guides the vocabulary, point of view, and the possible publisher of a work. Later, of course, the audience will determine strategies for marketing and distributing the book; the audience is significant whether writers market their own books or write a proposal or synopsis for an agent or acquisition editor.

Determining the Genre

When authors germinate ideas, they may not have a book in mind. They may have an idea that they want to express, to record and share with others. It may be a feeling prompted by an event—the birth of a child, a troubled relationship, death of a relative, crisis within a family, or any number of life events. The expression of that emotion and event may be expressed in a poem or short story, or it may form the beginning of a larger creative project: a book, play, or movie script. It may be fiction or nonfiction. a memoir or biography. All of these possibilities confront authors, but authors may decide to free their muse to guide them until the writing takes form.

With an audience in mind—perhaps thought of in very general terms—the author must consider the genre. Will this be a factual book—nonfiction—or a fictional portrayal influenced by real-life events? Is it a carefully researched biography of an individual's life, an account of the author's life (a memoir), or a completely fabricated story? If fiction, will it be a short story or a longer account—a novel? Or is it a compilation of poetry or short stories? Where would the book sit on the bookshelf in a bookstore or library?

Nonfiction fits into a variety of categories and audiences. This book, for example, is nonfiction and devoted to two audiences and how they can work together—writers and librarians. Our purpose is to help librarians in smaller libraries of all types to understand and participate in the book publishing process, and our audience includes writers who wish to self-publish. We have an audience in mind, and that audience guides our organization, vocabulary, and content. Similarly, the intended audience of a nonfiction work will guide the selection, depth, vocabulary, and organization of the whole. Decisions for a book intended for elementary school children will be far different than for a book on the same topic for a general adult population.

Audience matters for fiction, too, of course. Although a creative writer may let the characters respond to incidents and take the plot in directions not predetermined by the writer, the audience must be considered continuously, along with voice—the perspective of the storyteller. Because nonfiction requires careful planning, organization is our next consideration.

ORGANIZING NONFICTION

The genre of the work makes a big difference in how one proceeds early in the creative process. As already noted, if short stories or poetry are the products, the writing may proceed with little attempt to plan or to consider the larger work as a whole. The author of fiction can "let the creative juices flow" for days or even months as the project takes shape.

The creative process for nonfiction is different. Authors of history, biography, analysis of a subject, or a textbook must think about the total project early in the creative process. They must begin sketching the contents by outlining the major topics in the work. Making an outline of chapters with a summary of each chapter's content and a listing of topics in each chapter is a good exercise as the author constructs and organizes his work. The more complete the outline, the better for later work on the project. In other words, the writer "pays now or pays later"—the writer invests thought time in the organization of the material early or later, but it must be done.

The outline should be considered only a beginning, "written in pencil," to free the author's thinking, giving permission to make changes as the creative process continues. The outline is the skeleton that reviewing agents or editors will assess to determine the market for the book and to make the decision to publish or reject. Thinking through the intended audience and the need for this information is a critical component in the planning process. When an outline has been written, and authors believe that it represents the writing plan, they are ready to begin research and writing or to prepare a book synopsis or proposal.

BOOK SYNOPSIS OR PROPOSAL

If the book is a scholarly work or nonfiction with a limited audience and a commercial publisher is sought, a proposal might be prepared early in the creative process. The outline and synopsis of the book serve as a key element in the negotiation with an acquisition editor. For the beginning author of fictional works, biographies, or other topics considered for mass marketing, a literary agent is recommended by most experienced authors, and contact information for agents can be found in *Writers' Market* as well as online. Attendance at writing conferences also is a good source of information about literary agents. However, most agents require a completed manuscript before negotiating with an author. They want to know if the manuscript will appeal to a publisher. For that reason, agents are discussed in more depth later in this chapter.

In the nonfiction and limited market of professional and academic publishing and niche markets, acquisition editors may serve the dual role of recruiting authors for projects and acting as agents. The acquisition editor can review a proposal, suggest revisions, and serve as an advocate for the author when presenting the proposal to an editorial board. The acquisition editor plays an intermediary role between the publisher and the author.

A proposal or synopsis is an essential part of the planning process for a writing project. It forces writers to think through what they really want to accomplish. Another important point is that the proposal is negotiated up front, before the investment in time and energy to write an entire manuscript. Submitting finished manuscripts unsolicited to publishers is almost always a waste of time. Even when an author has a publishing record with a publisher or agent, a carefully prepared book proposal is the most effective way to present a project. Acquisition editors and agents want to know the concept in some detail before committing to a project.

The proposal is a key element in the publishing process. Publishers typically post on their Web site suggested formats for authors' book proposals. Libraries Unlimited, for example, suggests contacting an acquisition editor to review one's ideas (Libraries Unlimited 2015). Libraries Unlimited suggests including the following information in a proposal:

- Working title
- Purpose statement: explain the intent of the work, who it is for, and why it is needed
- Scope statement: describe the work's specific areas of coverage
- Objectives: identify the benefits readers will derive from the work
- Methodology: explain how you will research or compose the work
- Tentative outline: show how the work will be organized
- Competition or related works: identify similar titles and how your work will differ
- Approximate length (in pages or words)
- Resume or bio statement: describe why you are qualified to write this book

The above information is appropriate for nonfiction books, but the reader should consult the prospective publisher's Web site and/or an acquisition editor for specific advice for that publisher. Price (2010) provides very useful and explicit suggestions for preparing a book synopsis and a query letter that will portray a writer's work accurately and pique the interest of the editor or agent. Price also provides helpful hints for writing the author's biography that accompanies a submission. Some publishers actively seek writers and specify the series they're looking for; Harlequin (2015) on its Web site offers guidance to writers and suggests resources to consult.

Before accepting a proposal and issuing a contract, the publisher may request a writing sample, for example a draft book chapter, or a sample from a published work. A journal article or other previous publication also may be submitted to demonstrate the author's ability to write appropriately for the proposed project. Or, in the case of first-time authors, a portion or the entire manuscript may be required.

After the editorial board and decision makers for the publisher have rendered a decision, the acquisition editor will notify the author of suggested revisions, rejection, or acceptance of the proposal. When the publisher's representatives are satisfied with a proposal, a book contract will be issued.

Two authors of this book collaborated to submit a proposal for an earlier book (Grover et al. 2015) to their publisher in early winter, negotiated with content and title through the winter months, and agreed on a contract in the spring. A team of four co-authors proceeded with their writing of a first draft during the negotiation process. When the editorial committee approved the project, the author team had an accepted book outline, and the project was completed within the time agreed upon in the contract. From the time of the initial contact with the publisher until submission of the finished manuscript was two years.

The above example was a professional book by a lead author who had already published four books with this publishing house. The acquisition editor and decision makers at the publishing company knew his work. For general nonfiction, fiction, and poetry, writers who have no publishing record may need a completed manuscript before submitting a proposal or synopsis to a publisher.

WRITING AND RESEARCH

If the initial proposal is rejected, the search continues for a publisher. Whether the contract is issued, negotiations and revisions continue, or another publisher is sought, the author must continue to work on the project. Sometimes the proposal revision and negotiation process may continue for weeks or months before an agreement is reached. If no agreement is reached and no publisher is found, the writing still continues and the author then may consider self-publishing, which is described in Chapter 5.

When a proposal is rejected, the writing must continue with the confidence that the book will be published. The writing must continue because that's what writers do. True writers enjoy writing. They are driven to write, just as painters must paint and musicians must play their music. Artists must answer to their muse. Their art is not work—it's a gift that must be used and enjoyed, and it's a means of expression. It's what artists do, although joy is frequently mixed liberally with anxiety, frustration, and a dash of disappointment. As with many aspects of life—relationships, rearing children, and virtually any profession or occupation—there are emotional highs and lows that accompany progress. Progress is not an even progression—there are steps backward and to the side along the way. There is no "straight line" of progress when writing.

The authors of this book have many years' experience writing, working with publishers, and publishing with commercial publishers. It is rare to have a book proposal accepted immediately, although we have experienced that. We have also submitted proposals that have been rejected, and we have submitted a proposal that was revised twice before acceptance—a process that took several months, as described above. No matter the response of the publisher, writers must persist and believe in their work.

A Plan for Writing

Whether fiction, poetry, or nonfiction, the writing process should be a planned, intentional, continuous, and consistent activity. Successful writers are disciplined to the extent that they write on some kind of schedule. Writers who write when they "feel like it" often are not published writers. As mentioned above, writers must write. Writers are driven to write and feel incomplete if they don't. Even so, a writer should have a writing plan. If a morning person, the writer should schedule the most productive hours early in the day for writing.

For the majority of writers who are working at other jobs, that time may be early in the morning or late in the evening. Four of the co-authors of this book are employed full-time in libraries. One of the co-authors is retired and can devote more time and energy to the writing process, although he is an officer in a state association, is working on one other book project, and writes a regular op-ed column for his local daily newspaper.

Successful authors commit to writing for a certain period of time daily. It may be one hour before work or later in the evening. It may be the first hour or two hours of the day for a part-time writer or several hours for a full-time writer. Some successful authors who have other responsibilities at another unrelated job may cram writing into weekends and vacations in order to work intensively on a writing project at intervals. Regardless of the format, writing requires a planned commitment to the process. It's something we must do, but it can be exhausting, even frustrating. It saps one's physical, mental, and emotional energies. We may be unsatisfied with the results—but the next day or next week, it looks better than we remember. Then it feels good.

In a 1939 letter, Ernest Hemingway described the author's exhilaration when writing is going well:

> Have never known a summer to go so fast. When am working as hard as have been since the first week in April the days all just blur together. . . . Wake about seven thirty, have breakfast and am working by nine and usually work straight through until two p.m. After that it's like living in a vacuum until working time next day. (Phillips 1984, 53)

When the writing was not going well, Hemingway described his mood quite differently but offers solid advice in a letter to F. Scott Fitzgerald in 1929:

> You just have to *go on* when it is worst and most helpless—there is only one thing to do with a novel and that is go straight on through to the end of the damn thing. (Phillips 1984, 45)

Although Hemingway was referring to novel writing, the same advice applies to any type of writing: "go straight on through to the end of the damn thing."

Rewrite and Edit

Rewriting can occur as we work on the project according to our plan. When finished, the work should be edited as a totality to ensure continuity, to correct grammatical and factual errors, and to link related sections. Writing for publication requires review and revision throughout the process.

Unfortunately, we cannot trust ourselves in the editing and revision process. We need "other eyes" to read and review the work. That trusted person will identify errors and inconsistencies that we do not see. Our brain "sees" words the way they should be spelled (overlooking misspellings) and sentences the way we intended them (omitting words or explanatory information). We may be good writers and well educated, but we need the unbiased critical read of a trusted and reliable reader who will review the draft critically but constructively.

The trusted reader might be a spouse, friend, or colleague who can be trusted to read critically for grammar and meaning. The trusted reader may be a co-author, and one of the many advantages of team writing is the opportunity to test ideas and review with a colleague. Fiction writers often rely on "beta readers" on early drafts.

If the author is working on a contract with a commercial publisher, copyediting can be done as chapters are completed, or when the manuscript is complete. The acquisition editor will review for content and pass it to a copyeditor. Corrections may then be requested before the manuscript is forwarded through the publishing process.

However, the writer may also hire a professional copyeditor to review the manuscript. In that case, the editor should be screened carefully to understand the amount of editing experience and the intellectual background of the person. While people with editorial knowledge, skills, and experience are essential, it is also helpful to hire someone with knowledge of the genre and subject of the book. If fiction or poetry, a deep understanding of novels, short stories, or poetry should be in the editor's realm of experience. For nonfiction works, knowledge of the subject area can be very helpful. More discussion of copyediting is provided in Chapter 5.

How does the author locate a copyeditor? A local or state authors' group is a good source for information exchange on individuals qualified to edit and proofread a draft. The personal experience of other writers is invaluable. If the writer lives near a university, faculty or graduate students in the English or creative writing departments can be valuable sources for recommendations and expertise.

Still another source is *Writer's Digest* online. This extensive Web site provides names of copyeditors as well as writing aids. Workshops are also available, and cost varies according to the service provided. Nevertheless, *Writer's Digest* in print or online is a reputable source for writing support.

The first recourse should be the author's network of professional colleagues, friends, and fellow writers who might provide feedback and guidance or suggest reliable but knowledgeable friends and colleagues as the first choice for reading drafts. Also, writers' workshops may also invite participants to submit sample chapters for evaluation and suggestions. Advice from an experienced writer can be very helpful. We suggest joining a local authors' group to discuss writing and publishing issues. Your friends at the local public library can get you started.

PUBLISH THE MANUSCRIPT

With a completed manuscript, the author now must make a decision—try to publish through a commercial publisher or self-publish. The reasons for self-publishing are discussed in Chapter 5, but here we'll outline the issues to consider when the decision is to attempt to publish commercially.

Become Familiar with the Publishing Industry

A first step is to become familiar with the publishing industry, a fast-changing industry as noted in Chapter 1. A good recent source with interviews of agents, editors, book reviewers, and marketing people is Lynn Price's *The Writer's Essential Tackle Box: Getting a Hook on the Publishing Industry*. Whether submitting to an agent or to a small press, or self-publishing, the manuscript must be proofread and as error free as possible. Many, if not most, agents want to see a completed manuscript early in their negotiation with an author. If the writer has a track record, a proposal may be adequate. Neither agents nor editors have the time or patience to deal with a manuscript that looks amateurish.

Another reliable resource is *Writer's Digest*—the book (2015b) or Web site (2015a). The Web site is a comprehensive source for articles on the publishing process, agents, costs, and even courses to provide instruction on a variety of topics related to publishing your work.

WritersMarket.com, a division of the *Writer's Digest* Web site, provides lists of professional services that can help writers advance in their writing careers. Included are contests, conferences, professional services, self-publishing companies, organizations, education programs, and writing software. WritersMarket.com lists writing sources that pay for writers' work, and a paid subscription is required for access to this part of the Web site.

Writer's Digest Shop is a paid service that offers a critique of writing and includes a critique of a book proposal, synopsis, or manuscript. Editing services are available, and fees are charged as indicated on the Web site.

Publishers Marketplace is a Web site for writing and publishing professionals. Listed are agents, literary agencies, editors, writers, publicists, and consultants. An access fee is required.

A periodic visit to local bookstores is a good practice in order to stay current with new titles in your area of interest. Note the topics of books as well as their cover design and organization to get ideas. A bookstore is a display of current books that are on the market.

Large publishing houses seldom accept unsolicited manuscripts. These houses look to agents for new authors and titles. Smaller presses are more likely to accept unsolicited book proposals without going through agents. Depending on the book topic, a small press may be a good choice for a beginning author.

Literary Agents

For a writer of a work with a large potential audience, a literary agent is recommended. An agent will examine a manuscript (most require polished manuscripts before signing with an author) to gauge the publishing house most likely to want this book. The agent then shops the book to a publisher likely to have interest.

A good agent has developed relationships with a number of editors at publishing houses of various sizes and specialties. The agent is familiar with the market, and most publishing houses—certainly the larger ones—refuse to work directly with authors. The agent also assists the author in negotiating a publishing contract.

Unless writers have a friend in the business, they can find agents through sources like *Writer's Digest* or *Publishers Marketplace*. Good agents usually don't charge for reviewing and shopping a promising project, although they may require reimbursement for expenses. The agent's role is to connect with editors at publishing houses of varying sizes. A good agent has established relationships with editors in various sizes of publishing companies and is familiar with both the market and the niches of the various publishers. If the book has merit, an agent will find a suitable editor in a publishing house that would be interested in the book.

A useful source of information about agents, including interviews of successful agents, is found in Price's *The Writer's Essential Tackle Box* (2010). Price interviewed four established agents, who provide valuable insight into the agent's role and what a writer can expect from an agent. The chapter concludes with Price's summary and suggestions for authors considering agents.

When potential authors find names that they would like to consider, they should check the agent's Web site for their clientele and sales. Agents should be members of *Publishers Marketplace* and have a good sales record.

If soliciting an agent, a one-page synopsis of the book is a way to start communication, but some agents will demand a completed manuscript at the beginning of the inquiry process. The author should carefully outline the scope of the book and its attractive features, and might mention the intended audience and how this book is a unique contribution to the market. Agents and publishers want something that's going to appeal to an audience—something that will sell. Agents can be contacted by e-mail, and many will respond within days or a few weeks, but they are busy people.

If an agent is enlisted and that person finds an interested publisher, the book proposal will be directed to the publisher's acquisition committee, which may be comprised of editors and marketing people. These professionals are looking for a well-written proposal, and later a manuscript, that will appeal to an audience. The work should be unique and fulfill a need in the marketplace.

Another factor for publishers is what the author can contribute to promotion. Does the author have a Web page and a presence on social media in order to help promote the book?

Book Shepherds

If authors want to self-publish, they may want to consider a book shepherd, usually a costly choice. Authors who want to control all aspects of publication but have little or no experience will want advice from an experienced pro. These consultants are for hire and can be vital resources for authors who have a budget that can afford this level of consulting. Price (2010) devotes a chapter to book shepherds and provides interviews with two. Shepherds coordinate all aspects of book production and guide the author away from costly mistakes, but at a price that could be several hundred dollars per hour. However, there are alternatives that are less expensive for those willing to accept the responsibility, as we discuss in later chapters.

For more detailed information about book shepherds, see Price (2010, 95–114) and go to the Writer's Digest Web site to see author-consulting services available.

Acquisition Editors

When the writer feels confident that the draft is ready for outside review, the manuscript can be submitted to an agent, as noted above. For niche markets, for example professional and scholarly works, an acquisition editor could be contacted. Knowledge of a publisher's focus is important in order to identify a publisher that might be interested in your work; contacting the publisher can be the first step in contacting an acquisition editor. Browse publishers' Web pages to determine names of acquisition editors and the format for an inquiry.

The acquisition editor can be both dependable critic and advocate for advancing the project to publication. The acquisition editor has a stake in the manuscript because that person has reviewed the book proposal and submitted it for editorial review before a contract is issued. Acquisition editors want to see books published, but they also want quality publications. Their considerable experience as authors and editors is put into practice when they read and evaluate the finished manuscript.

Acquisition editors will forgive details like conformity to style for references, although they are mindful of such errors. They assess the book for organization, clarity, accuracy, and flow of the manuscript, regardless of genre. They will contact authors if revisions are necessary, and it is possible that a rewrite of sections might be required.

When the acquisition editor accepts the manuscript, it is passed to a copyeditor who does a careful review of spelling, grammar, and style that conforms to the requirements of the publisher. The review is detailed and comprehensive, and the copyeditor may have questions of the author before passing the project on in the publishing process—layout and cover design. The author may have little or no input in these processes.

The copyeditor submits the edited manuscript for author review. At this point in the publication process, only minor revisions are accepted—changed dates or citation corrections. Revision of sentences or paragraphs is not expected or permitted. The content is "locked in" at this point.

A proofreader is engaged at this point to read the final manuscript after the acquisition editor and copyeditor have finished their work. The copyeditor checks for typographical errors, inconsistencies, and misspellings. The proofreader generally conducts the last review after all changes have been made in the manuscript. This review typically occurs after the copyeditor, in consultation with the author, has made revisions to correct grammar errors and style inconsistencies. The proofreader also reviews the front and back matter before the manuscript goes to press.

FINAL STAGES

Concurrently with the above processes, the publishing staff is designing the layout and the book cover. A designer or design editor designs the book covers, interior, and jacket (if necessary) for a book. This person also may be involved in designing promotional materials for the book.

Marketing staff is responsible for promoting a book through advertising in newspapers, magazines, journals, and media that will reach the intended audience. Marketing may include display, sales, and author signings in bookstores and at author fairs and professional conferences. Marketing personnel may submit a questionnaire to the author as they prepare marketing copy. They request information about the author and a description of the book's content, as well as the intended audience. This information is then integrated into the marketing plan for the book.

A few weeks after copyediting, the page proofs are sent from the publisher to the author for review. Only minor corrections are allowed. The author is given a date for returning the page proofs, and the book is ready for publication.

At this point, the publisher may contract an indexer for a nonfiction book, or the author may have the expertise to create an index. The layout design and cover are finished, and the book is ready for printing and binding.

The publisher then implements its program for distribution, sales, marketing, and publicity after the book is printed and bound. After publication, and within one year, the publisher issues payment of royalties to the author according to the agreement in the contract.

All of these processes are a great service to the author. If a book is self-published, of course, the author is responsible for coordinating or providing all of the processes outlined above, and they are discussed in Chapters 5, 6, 7, and 8.

Commercial publishers provide expertise in editing, design, printing, distribution, and marketing—all part of their service. There is a charge for this service, of course. Typically a publisher pays the author 10 to 12 percent of the sales—in other words, the publisher retains about 90 percent of the revenue for the publisher's services. For all of the services offered, the cost enables the author to devote her time and energy to writing or other activities. Before self-publishing, the writer should be aware of the knowledge and experience afforded by publishers and the benefits of publishers' services.

CHAPTER SUMMARY

The author should be aware of book publishing stages whether or not a commercial publisher will be sought. The publisher provides valuable expertise in the editing, design, indexing, printing, distribution, and marketing of a book. The wise author, like a chess player or administrator, must plan ahead for the total process of book publishing as the book is written.

Planning early in the process is important for an author. The elements of a typical book proposal provide an outline for the author to follow and encourage the author to consider the intended audience and marketing. The intended audience, while valuable for marketing, is an essential ingredient in the decision-making process as the author is writing.

When the manuscript is complete, the author must make a decision to acquire an agent, to submit a book proposal to an acquisition editor at a publishing house, or to self-publish. Chapters 4 and 5 explore the processes that must be assumed when the decision is made to self-publish.

REFERENCES

Grover, Robert J., Roger C. Greer, Herbert K. Achleitner, and Kelly Visnak. 2015. *Evolving Global Information Infrastructure and Information Transfer*. Santa Barbara, CA: Libraries Unlimited.

Harlequin Books. 2015. "Write for Harlequin." http://www.harlequin.com/articlepage.html?articleId=538&chapter=0. Accessed December 14, 2015.

Libraries Unlimited. 2015. "Become an Author; Submit Your Proposal." http://www.abc-clio.com/LibrariesUnlimited/Authors/BecomeanAuthor.aspx.

Phillips, Larry W., ed. 1984. *Ernest Hemingway on Writing*. New York: Scribner.

Price, Lynn. 2010. *The Writer's Essential Tackle Box: Getting a Hook on the Publishing Industry*. Lake Forest, CA: Behler Publications.

Publishers Marketplace. 2015. http://www.publishersmarketplace.com. Accessed December 16, 2015.

Writer's Digest. 2015a. http://www.writersdigest.com. Accessed December 16, 2015.

Writer's Market 2016. 2015b. Robert Lee Brewer, ed. Cincinnati, OH: Writer's Digest Books.

Writer's Market. 2015. http://www.writersmarket.com. Accessed December 16, 2015.

Yager, Fred, and Jan Yager. 2005. *Career Opportunities in the Publishing Industry*. New York: Ferguson/Facts on File.

$$4$$

TRADITIONAL PUBLISHING

CHAPTER OVERVIEW

Writing a book is something many people want to do, but writing the book and seeing it published are time-consuming, laborious tasks. This chapter describes the traditional processes involved in publishing a book commercially so that the reader has a realistic understanding of the time, effort, and plain hard work that must be invested in writing and publishing a book.

Chapter 3 outlined the thought processes involved in planning a book, whether for self-publishing or for submission to a commercial publisher. In this chapter the stages of book publishing are described after the manuscript is completed. A publisher provides valuable expertise in the editing, design, indexing, printing, distribution, and marketing of a book—processes that an author assumes when self-publishing.

When the manuscript is complete, the author must make a decision to acquire an agent, submit a book proposal to an acquisition editor at a publishing house, or self-publish. This chapter explores the processes associated with commercial publishing and those processes that must be assumed when the decision is made to self-publish. We'll also look more closely at the services that publishers provide, including book design, as well as the printing process, distribution, promotion, and marketing.

COMMERCIAL PUBLISHERS

When we think of publishers, we usually think of the big publishing houses—for example, Penguin Random House, Scribner, or Doubleday—and we think of New York as the home of these publishers. Those of us wanting to author the next best-selling novel that becomes a blockbuster movie think immediately of these publishing houses; however, the publishing scene is much more complex, and various publishing options currently are available, including print-on-demand and vanity presses in their various forms.

In recent years the large publishing houses, responding to the technological revolution in book publishing, have merged into a few conglomerates—often international in their reach. These publishers are not only big names in publishing, they have big budgets, and their print runs may be tens of thousands to more than a million. This is large-scale publishing for the big-name popular authors who are on the *New York Times* bestseller lists.

These huge publishing houses are few in number, and many publishing companies have merged in recent years as the industry has been transformed by the technological revolution. There remain a large number of smaller and independent trade publishers that have much smaller cash flows, and the technological change that encouraged the merger of publishing houses has also enabled the creation of small presses, more vanity presses, and self-publishing. These independent publishers work on a much smaller scale, releasing fewer titles and specializing in certain genres (e.g., mysteries, memoirs, romance, and nonfiction in certain categories). These smaller presses have smaller staffs and may outsource services, including distribution and marketing.

To learn of the many publishing possibilities available, the reader is urged to consult a recent edition of *Writer's Market 2016* (2015) or visit the Web site.

BOOK DESIGN

Commercial publishers handle the design of a book, and the author should be aware of those book sections that are very familiar to librarians but which readers and authors may overlook. For that reason, we'll review here the textual features of a book.

Cover

Booksellers and bookstore workers are well aware that the book's cover can make the difference between selling the book and leaving it on the shelf to collect dust. Since smaller-run books are often softcover, the covers can be as colorful and eye-catching as the slick book jackets of hardcover books that cost much more. The design and title should not only describe the concepts in the book but also entice the browser into picking up the book and possibly buying it. Indeed, a browser *should* be able to tell a book by its cover.

The front cover appearance should draw the reader's attention so that she picks up the book and either flips through the pages or turns to the back cover; when that happens, the cover has done its job. The back cover should communicate more about the content and entice the reader to open the book. The cover must sell book reviewers, distributors, and bookstore and library customers, or they won't pick up a book to look inside.

The book title is part of that first impression of the book. The title should suggest the content and do so in a concise and clever manner. Take the time to consider a title that is descriptive and memorable. If necessary, a subtitle can be used to bring clarity to a brief title.

Type font on the cover and title page should be selected to be consistent with the topic and tone of the book, but beware that an attempt to use a unique font may be more distracting than a plainer, more familiar font. Sometimes an attempt to be creative is a distraction and becomes a negative feature of the book design. The title should be bold and easily read at a glance.

A brief biography of the author to indicate her qualifications for writing the book is a standard feature of a back cover, along with some testimonials by knowledgeable persons. These testimonials help market the book.

Illustrations are an important element of a book cover. Commercial publishers frequently have illustrators on staff, or they may outsource cover design to artists who can create an appealing drawing, photograph, or other design that will attract reader attention and suggest book content. Few authors have the artistic skill to design effective book covers, although word processing programs provide clip art and features that enable a writer to create attractive and professional-looking illustrations.

Graphic artists complete the cover by selecting fonts and arranging the verbiage to attract the attention of the reader. The book title is extremely important in this presentation of the book at a glance. We want to emphasize that the cover should suggest the subject and tone of the book to draw the reader's attention.

Title Page

After one or two blank pages, the reader encounters the book's title page, which includes the significant identification information: author's (and all co-authors') full name(s), full title, publisher's name and place(s) of publication.

On the back (verso) side of the title page is other important information: copyright date, copyright owner, ISBN (International Standard Book Number), and cataloging information. Copyright date is the date the book is copyrighted upon its completion. The copyright owner may be the author or the book publisher. The International Standard Book Number is a unique 13-digit number assigned to each edition of a book. In the United States, R. R. Bowker Company issues ISBNs for a fee. The cataloging information is usually provided by commercial publishers that request cataloging by the Library of Congress, including the Dewey Decimal Classification number, Library of Congress number, and subject headings assigned by the Library of Congress, which attempts to catalog and store every book published in the United States.

Librarians expect this information to be uniform as they process books for their collections and prepare them for the library shelves. Commercial publishers routinely provide this information, and authors who self-publish should also.

Dedication

Authors usually want to recognize those special people who have tolerated the ups and downs associated with book authoring. This is often a spouse, partner, or loved one who has tolerated the author through his many moods and has provided emotional and perhaps financial support during the birthing process of this work. Others who have influenced or inspired the author in some way are identified in the dedication.

Acknowledgments

The acknowledgments section is usually longer and more detailed than the dedication, listing the people who have contributed ideas, influenced the writing in some way, and offered some help editing, proofreading, or in some ways helping the author complete the work.

Preface

When the manuscript is complete, the author can provide background information about the book to her readers. For nonfiction books, the author may wish to explain the intended audience, scope of the book, its organization, and special features. She may relate the inspiration for the book and how the ideas germinated. She may also relate the people and events that contributed to the formation of the final product and acknowledge the contributions of specific people in lieu of an acknowledgments section. The preface provides the author an opportunity to "vent" and explain influences that resulted in the book in its final form. Typically fiction books do not include a preface unless a literary scholar is introducing a new or special edition of a classic.

Table of Contents

Although fiction books may not have a listing of chapters, a table of contents is essential for nonfiction books, listing the chapter titles, chapter sections, and accompanying page numbers. The table of contents assists the reader in determining the value of the book and in locating information of interest. The table of contents is the result of the careful planning and outlining of the book as described in Chapter 3. It is a reference point for the reader as he locates pertinent sections for his reading, and the table of contents can help a browser determine if she will read the book and purchase it.

List of Illustrations

Another book guide for nonfiction is the list of illustrations. Along with the table of contents, this section can guide the reader to points of interest that facilitate retrieval of information. Illustrations are important additions that authors must carefully consider when writing and designing a book.

Introduction and Text

The introductory chapter, usually written after other chapters are finished, provides an overview for nonfiction books, introducing key concepts to be found in the various chapters. Fiction and poetry also must have carefully crafted introductory chapters to engage the reader immediately and to guide the reader into the enjoyment that awaits.

Appendices

Works of any genre may have appendices that provide additional pertinent information to support textual material. Fiction, especially historical fiction, may include maps, illustrations, chronologies, or historical anecdotes that augment the text.

Bibliography

Nonfiction books typically include a bibliography of selected further reading on the book's topic. Many of the titles may be included in chapter bibliographies, and additional titles may be suggested. Annotations to guide the reader may be included.

Index

An index of names, titles, and subjects is essential for a nonfiction book. The index and table of contents are the primary means by which a reader can locate specific information. The index is so important that an author may wish to hire a professional indexer.

Interior Design

As indicated above, design begins with the book cover—and a reader should indeed be able to determine the content by looking at it; the cover is a marketing device that invites a browser, book reviewer, or distributor to pick up the book. The choice of colors, the graphic design, and the font should communicate the content and tone of the book. Colors and fonts suggest moods and frames of mind; be certain that the outward appearance reflects the intent and character of the text. For a thoughtful discussion of design by a skilled graphic artist, see Price (2010, 127–140).

The book design includes the appearance of each page—type font selected, margins, heading size and placement, and white space. The appearance of the font should be consistent with the visual and spiritual theme of the book. A wide variety of type fonts are available, and the designers at a publishing house, if they're doing their job effectively, will consider the font as carefully as the page layout.

We've already discussed the importance of a table of contents for browsing and finding information; the browser most likely will check the table of contents before purchasing a nonfiction book.

EDITING

The editing process is both essential and expensive for the publisher. Typically, an acquisition editor has screened the content of a manuscript before sending it to the line editor, whose job is to read carefully for comprehension—does the content make sense to the reader? In some cases, especially for nonfiction and scholarly works, an editor may submit the manuscript to trusted scholars in the field to review the content. Then the in-house editor may elect to work with the writer to rewrite for clarity and logical organization. The purpose is to revise a manuscript so that it reads logically and understandably.

Throughout the editing process the author must set aside her ego. This work that represents an investment of countless hours, late nights, exhausting rewrites, fits of depression, restarts, rewording, and rethinking can become as near and dear to the author as a friend—even a child. Our loyal dog may not have earned the loyalty this manuscript elicits from the writer. Nevertheless, in order to move the project forward, it is necessary to confront changes to this near-masterpiece. The author must face this prospect and deal with it. Asked to revise, the author's best response is, "Of course I can do that." If there is a good reason for retaining certain elements of style or arrangement of the parts (order), they can be stated, and the author's rationale may prevail; however, an author must be willing to entertain an outsider's reaction to the work. New authors especially must be prepared for critique and revision.

Another type of editing—by other editors in-house or outsourced—is done by copyeditors, who carefully read a manuscript for details—spelling, grammar, punctuation, capitalization, style consistency, and general integrity of the writing. When this type of editing is complete, the publisher returns the edited manuscript to the author for approval. At this point, the author can review all edits and possibly refuse revisions that seem to change the intended meaning of sentences. Typically, the author has the final decision during the editing process, although the author may not make substantive changes in the text at this point in the publishing process, especially when changes may add to or take away from the number of pages under contract for the book.

After the author has approved the manuscript, the design team assembles the page proofs—a digitized representation of the book's pages as they will appear after publication. These page proofs are e-mailed to the author for final review for typographical errors; no other revisions are permitted at this stage. The author is granted a specific amount of time to complete the review because the publishing calendar has been set, and the print run has been scheduled.

PRINTING

At this point the book cover and pages are printed, cut, and assembled. Technology advances in the last 20 years have provided more options for publishing. It is now financially feasible, using digital publishing techniques, to print smaller press runs, providing publishers and authors many more options for printing.

The large publishing houses print thousands of copies for a press run and may issue thousands more in hardback, paperback, and as e-books. Most publishing now accommodates both digital and paper formats. New technologies have enabled print-on-demand and have expanded the options for authors who want to publish in nontraditional ways.

Print-on-Demand (POD)

Print-on-demand publishers make copies based on orders received. Digital printing allows publishers to accumulate orders and have them in hand before the costly printing process. Here's where the large trade publishers have an advantage; they have the cash reserves so that, based on experience in the marketplace, they can hire top-notch artists for cover design and knowledgeable and experienced editors to guarantee a quality product. With the limited budgets of print-on-demand small presses, the quality of design and editing may be less than ideal.

The same factors are at work in book distribution and marketing. Because POD printers have small budgets, they cannot afford a sales force or expensive marketing and advertising budgets. Although trade publishers may send scores, even hundreds, of advance reader copies to book reviewers and large bookstore headquarters staff, smaller presses typically do not provide large-scale distribution of sample copies.

Consequently, the low-budget world of POD publishers requires them to focus on their chief market—authors who market, promote, and sell their own books. The POD publishers provide discounts based on the number of books sold, and authors can then afford to buy more books. Another advantage to the POD publishers is that they offer no return policy; the books sold to authors stay sold and are not returned. In the POD marketplace, all of the expense and risk is placed on the authors.

In summary, POD publishing is tilted in favor of the publishers so that they have much less risk than trade publishers. They need little or no marketing or sales force, and they can have a small editorial staff or hire editing on a contractual basis. Overhead is low, and the key factor for success is a solid author base to buy the books.

Vanity/Subsidized Printing

Commercial publishers assume the cost and the risk of the publishing process; some even provide authors advance royalties when they sign contracts. These advances are the exception for the big-name popular authors who sell millions of copies of their books. Most authors are happy to see their titles in print and to receive a small royalty check annually.

For those authors willing to pay to have their books published, vanity presses are there to publish an author's project for pay. These presses received their names because they cater to the author's vanity, who wants to see his precious work in print, and the vanity press has been around as long as there have been authors and publishers willing to take the author's money.

In today's publishing milieu, there are many opportunities for authors to solicit assistance in publishing their work. A number of print-on-demand (POD) publishers and self-publishing services help authors publish their work for a fee. Many provide "review" of manuscripts, but the question is whether the review is truly an evaluation of the work from a seasoned editor's point of view—or whether the "review" is a pro forma positive endorsement of every manuscript to encourage publishing at the author's expense.

A variety of such services are available. Our caution to authors is the familiar warning, "buyer beware." Before signing a contract, the author should understand completely the services provided and the costs. Print-on-demand and vanity publishers are in business to make money from authors wanting to publish, and their assistance in marketing and distributing the book should be scrutinized carefully as well as the number of books that the author will receive for the fees charged. In today's publishing industry, the distinction between print-on-demand and vanity presses is blurred.

Librarians have been aware of vanity presses for many years—possibly since the invention of the printing press. As noted above, the editing, design, printing, distribution, and promotion of books is an expensive enterprise. The big trade publishers invest in large press runs (tens of thousands) and multimedia promotion of their books. Consequently, they are very judicious in the titles they elect to publish. That's why they don't bother with unsolicited manuscripts and depend on agents who know the market to help in the winnowing process. It's rare for a novice writer to snag a contract with one of the big-name trade publishers, although it does happen—almost always with an agent. While it's a writer's dream to have a book published by a big New York house, a writer may want to break into print another way.

Because engaging a publisher for a book is a long shot—better odds than winning a lottery, but not much—vanity presses arose to address the publishing desires of writers. The term "vanity press," as you may guess, suggests that some writers believe they have written a book that the world is looking for, and they are willing to pay for its publication. The term has a negative connotation, and librarians have been wary of such publishing houses. When reviewing books, librarians look for reliable publishing imprints because publishing houses are careful to protect their brand name, knowing that book buyers associate quality with their name. That reputation and name recognition translates into sales and profits, and publishers don't want to lose money. Likewise, librarians work with limited budgets and look for quality books to purchase; a publisher's name is one variable that librarians consider when evaluating a book.

Vanity presses have removed the gamble from book publishing—they don't worry about sales volume because they rely upon the author to pay for the cost of printing. Both sides are happy; the publisher has a known quantity to print, and there's no worry about promotion costs. The author is happy because she comes away with a published book without the hassle of agents, delays in the review process, and the nasty rejection letters. The vanity press is a shortcut to seeing one's work in published form.

Of course, there's a price to pay for the design, editing, and printing of a book. Then there's the promotion, which takes a great deal of time and money to get the book into bookstores. Since many independent bookstores have gone out of business, unable to compete with the large chains like Barnes and Noble or Amazon, placement in a local independent bookstore or boutique is the most likely possibility, but sales may be limited. Printing the books is only the first, albeit expensive, step in selling a book to the public awaiting your great work.

Digital technologies have made possible the print-on-demand printers and subsidized publishers who offer a variety of services for a price. The wise author who takes this route must be wary and ask questions to understand and assess the services offered by the publisher. Remember: the subsidized publisher or vanity press makes its profit on the author, and the quality of the work and the sales of a book are the author's responsibility and expense.

DISTRIBUTING

The task of getting the finished book from the publisher to book reviewers, bookstores, libraries, online sales, and approval plans is assigned to the book distributor. Book distributors provide a list of many publishers' titles, providing a simpler purchasing service for bookstores and libraries so that book buyers can purchase from one source instead of working with a large number of publishers.

The large publishing houses have sales teams that know the market and sales outlets. Through catalogs and sales representatives, publishers present the titles of their many imprints to book retailers and wholesalers. Smaller presses may sign on with independent distributors who have working relationships with booksellers in niche markets. Some of these distribution companies distribute other items, and some sell directly to the public.

Bookstores are the main outlet for selling books, and the independent, owner-operated bookstores still exist, but the bookselling business is dominated by the large chains, for example, Amazon and Barnes and Noble. Bookstores usually sell other printed matter, including a selection of newspapers and magazines. Colleges and universities may have their own student bookstore on campus that specializes in textbooks for courses and scholarly books. Large chains often own bookstores on college campuses.

In traditional publishing, approximately 90 percent of a book's sales go to the publishing house or subsidiaries responsible for distribution and marketing. Here are approximate costs for traditional book publishing gathered from various sources:

- 10–15 percent to the author (royalties)
- 10 percent to the wholesaler
- 10 percent for printing (this is usually subcontracted out)
- 45 percent to the retailer
- 7 percent for marketing
- 10–15 percent for editing, design, and preproduction

New technologies like the e-book have introduced electronic publishing to the distribution process, although the processes and cost for e-book publication are similar to that of traditional paper books. However, technology also makes possible print-on-demand, which has many adaptations for authors' consideration when self-publishing. These variations are described in Chapters 5, 6 and 8.

PROMOTION AND MARKETING

Getting the finished book to readers is the next step in the publishing process. Although commercial publishers assume this responsibility, the author still plays a role. Typically the marketing personnel ask the author to provide information about the book contents, intended audience, unique features of the book, and perhaps reviewing sources. This query of the author is done six to twelve months before the book is printed and released.

Publishers usually control the advertising and marketing, but they may subcontract to marketing agencies. Smaller publishers may also subcontract editing, proofreading, design, and other aspects of the production process to freelance specialists. In-house salespeople also may be replaced by companies that specialize in sales to bookstores and chain stores for a fee.

Publishers of all sizes produce catalogs, list their titles on Web sites, and promote sales at professional conferences at the state, regional, and national levels. Publishers buy advertising in library professional journals and periodicals that reach the intended audience. The high-volume publishers advertise on mass media—popular magazines in print and online, newspapers, television, and online. The American Library Association mid-winter and summer conferences are showcases for the library marketplace, and there are regularly scheduled conferences for ALA divisions like the American Association of School Librarians, Public Library Association, and Association of College and Research Libraries. Publishers budget for the marketing of books, and authors also can promote their titles through their own networks.

Authors can assist with marketing by publishing a related article in a professional journal or other type of periodical. Presenting at conferences and participating in book signings also helps to market the book. Using social media is now a significant part of the marketing; an author's Web page is an important marketing tool.

In summary, the author intent on placing her book with readers must think about marketing strategies throughout the writing process. Familiar and frequently repeated advice to authors is "write about something you're passionate about"; that same passion should be applied to getting the book into the hands of readers. If an author believes her book is important, she should play an active role in marketing the book. It's what professional writers do.

AUTHOR AS PUBLISHER

Many beginning authors either have received numerous rejections from publishers or are unwilling to go through the laborious, time-consuming, and ego-testing process of submitting their work to publishers and/or agents. Stories abound of authors who have submitted their works to publishers, waited several months for a response, and finally received the manuscript back *unread*. Stories of an author who found an agent and was successful publishing a first book and selling hundreds of thousands of copies are true, but they are the exception.

With the technology available today, the publishing process is available to writers to make self-publishing affordable—even profitable. But the aspiring author must be aware of the processes involved in order to see her work in final published form. The chapters that follow take us through these stages of book production.

Publishers take a great load off the shoulders of writers by performing these needed services—the editing, printing, distribution, and marketing. Authors who self-publish take on a much heavier, time-consuming, and costly burden. We present more details of these processes in Chapters 5, 6, 7, and 8.

CHAPTER SUMMARY

Publishing a book is a complex task that offers many challenges to the writer. In this chapter we described the traditional processes involved in publishing a book commercially so that writers can understand and appreciate the role of publishers. When self-publishing, the author assumes all of the roles of a publisher, including the editing, design, indexing, printing, distribution, and marketing of the book.

When a manuscript is complete, the author must decide whether to acquire an agent and submit the manuscript for commercial publishing or pursue self-publishing. Submitting to a commercial publisher is a time-consuming process that often ends in rejection. Access to new technology now gives writers the opportunity to assume roles that publishers traditionally have filled.

Chapter 5 explores the tasks and challenges that an author faces when she assumes the role of book publisher.

REFERENCES

Price, Lynn. 2010. *The Writer's Essential Tackle Box: Getting a Hook on the Publishing Industry.* Lake Forest, CA: Behler Publications.
Writer's Market 2016. 2015. Robert Lee Brewer, ed. Cincinnati, OH: Writer's Digest Books.
Writer's Market. 2015. WritersMarket. http://www.writersmarket.com.

SELF-PUBLISHING A BOOK

CHAPTER OVERVIEW

This chapter is written to guide authors and the librarians who assist them in evaluating the suitability of material for self-publishing. It will also illuminate the many processes in self-publishing and challenge misperceptions of the legitimacy of self-publishing and the effort required to succeed. Self-publishing means taking on the role of writer as a small business, which translates into a big investment of time and effort.

The process of publishing a book and getting it into readers' hands is a rapidly shifting model that is affecting change for writers, publishers, libraries, and readers. Self-publishing is more affordable and accessible than ever before, and many writers are eliminating the middleman and submitting their work for reader approval through the open market. Savvy companies are competing to cash in on the self-publishing boom by offering writers new programs and platforms for printing and sharing their work. Writers, libraries, and publishing companies can hardly keep up because profit models, contract terms, and licensing options are evolving as quickly as anyone can read the details in the fine print.

OVERCOMING THE STIGMA OF SELF-PUBLISHING

Self-publishing is a concept that comes with baggage. Many readers and librarians equate self-published work with poorly edited writing and low-quality book design and printing, even now, at a time when successful self-published writers are scoring traditional book contracts and movie deals. Often, self-publishing is viewed as a last resort for authors who were unable to connect with an agent or market their work for sale with traditional publishing houses. Part of this stigma no doubt originated in recent history due to the products of "vanity presses," which often profited by printing and selling large quantities of subpar work to writers who had no other avenue to publication. Today, self-publishing authors who jump to market without a thorough editing, peer review, and revision process contribute to a lingering bad reputation for self-published work.

The history of self-publishing is much richer and more admirable than readers realize, having long been an avenue for authors to publish literature of merit that was not considered a good commercial investment for publishing houses. Jane Austen paid to publish *Sense and Sensibility* with a vanity press, and Walt Whitman designed and published *Leaves of Grass*. Marcel Proust published *Swann's Way* on his own dime, and Virginia Woolf started a small press, Hogarth, to publish her work and that of other authors (Fitzgerald 2013). A current example of a successful indie publisher is Small Beer Press, founded in 2000 by author Kelly Link and her husband, Gavin J. Grant. Small Beer publishes collections and novels by authors including Kij Johnson and Karen Joy Fowler, as well as the fiction 'zine *Lady Chatterley's Rosebud Wristlet*, which has featured work by Ursula Le Guin and Joan Aiken (Grant 2015).

Today's self-published authors are part of a noble tradition of enterprising, persistent writers who knew that they had something of value to contribute to the readers of the world, even if a publisher did not readily agree. While we can be sure that only a small fraction of the many works self-published since the invention of movable type continue to be read today, the same could be said of traditionally published titles. The distribution game is changing with e-books and print-on-demand, giving self-published titles and small presses increased legitimacy and marketability, and giving authors better odds of reaching their audience than ever before.

WHY SELF-PUBLISH?

As previously noted, technology is changing rapidly, with new innovations daily that allow information to be shared faster, farther, and with less expense. The publishing industry and the business of writing can change as a result. While self-publishing was once an alternative publishing path available to the few with both ambition and funding, technology has leveled the playing field. If a writer knows about the resources available and has time to invest, she can publish work inexpensively with tools available at most public libraries or as part of most home office setups.

Mark Coker (2014), founder of Smashwords, sees an "e-book self-publishing revolution" in the works. Coker predicts that "decades from now, e-book self-publishing will be viewed by historians as no less transformative than the advent of the Gutenberg printing press." The opportunity to make a book available to anyone on earth who has access to an Internet-connected screen is indeed revolutionary.

The International Data Corporation (2015) predicts that 1.9 billion smartphones will be in use around the world by the year 2019. For authors who publish in e-book format, this translates into the potential to reach thousands of readers, whenever and wherever they are.

Many writers and readers already recognize the historic transformation occurring around us, which is the reason librarians can benefit from learning more about self-publishing. For better or worse, e-book publishing gives writers the ability to publish work rapidly to respond to reader demand, cultural trends, or effective sales techniques. Readers can discover a new author and buy additional books in minutes, paying with credit card and accessing the book digitally from their own device from anywhere in the world. Just as copying books by hand was a time-consuming process compared to the advance of the printing press, so is the traditional publisher timeline of bringing an accepted manuscript to market compared to new, faster publishing methods.

Print-on-demand also has changed this landscape for authors who want printed copies of their books available to sell themselves, or to distribute for ordering worldwide. Instead of running a personal warehouse from a garage, authors can upload their manuscripts to a print-on-demand service like CreateSpace and make their works available for sale through Amazon.com at no cost or risk to themselves for the outlay of printing costs.

While some authors will choose to focus exclusively on either e-books or print-on-demand titles, most authors will want to offer their books in both of these popular reading formats. Successful self-publishing authors who are making a small business or full-time effort of their writing will want to consider audiobooks, author Web sites, book tours, and speaking engagements. This publishing model has changed so quickly that the support services for authors haven't developed quickly enough to catch the demand and interest.

Here, then, is an opportunity for librarians to do what they do best—guide the writers of their communities in learning about the information, services, and technology that can help them succeed as published authors, helping them gain necessary skills and make informed choices that work for their projects. By doing so, librarians can enhance their engagement with a portion of the people that they serve, while supporting content creation that resonates with readers, who are still their biggest library supporters. As advances in word processing made typing manuscripts more accessible to more potential writers, advances in publishing and distribution enable bringing a book to market independently more desirable and attainable to potential writers. Demand is expected to increase for knowledge of and access to these tools. As noted previously, it's also the perfect way for a librarian to stay at the forefront of publishing innovations. It's a win for everyone involved.

IS SELF-PUBLISHING RIGHT FOR YOUR BOOK?

Not all work is appropriate for traditional publishing. In fact, there are projects that seem ideal for self-publishing. For example, as mentioned in Chapter 2, micropublishing is a great fit when smaller quantities are desired for a smaller audience, such as books written for a niche market or for a regional audience. Books that mix genres are another good example. Traditional publishers may shy away from work that seems to resist existing marketing templates.

When deciding how to publish a book, the first question should be, "Who are the readers?" Before deciding how a work should be published and shared with readers, take the time to consider carefully the intended audience and how they are likely to access your work.

Once an audience is targeted, do the research to determine how books are promoted and marketed to those readers. Think about the genre where the book fits best, then read books published in that genre. Consider which formats are most popular in the genre—hardback, trade paperback, mass-market paperback, e-book, or audiobook. Browse the bestsellers, the hidden gems, and the classics. Investigate distribution to see the difference in the genre according to your local bookstore inventory, major online retailers, major e-book retailers, and library print and online collections. Read the publishing trends articles, as well as book reviews from libraries and popular blogs. Know which books might be used as a basis for comparison, either favorably or unfavorably.

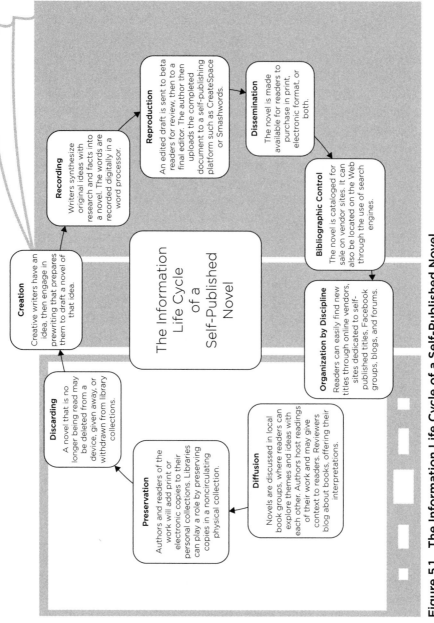

Figure 5.1   The Information Life Cycle of a Self-Published Novel

Source: Greer, Roger C., Robert J. Grover, and Susan G. Fowler. 2013. *Introduction to the Library and Information Professions.* 2nd ed. Santa Barbara, CA: Libraries Unlimited.

> **Consider the Following Questions for the Book's Genre:**
> - What are the best sellers?
> - What are the books that professional critics and reviewers rate highly?
> - Which books have great ratings and reviews from readers on Web sites such as Goodreads or Amazon?
> - Are the hot titles in the book's genre predominantly published or self-published, or is there a good mix? (In the romance genre there is clearly an audience of readers who are open to self-published titles, for example.)
> - Are there awards in the genre? If so, which books are winning them? Are they the same books that are popular with readers?

If an author's book doesn't fit neatly into a genre or isn't comparable to anything else, that doesn't mean she shouldn't publish. Actually, that could be a very good reason to choose self-publishing. Work that doesn't fit the current trends or popular genres may not be as likely to be picked up by a mainstream publishing house, but that does not mean that it lacks literary merit. If the work is an outlier, the author should consider who will want to read it and how the reader will find it and purchase it. A self-published author's path to publication may include more trial and error in marketing and distribution than that of an author who is able to chart a potential path to success through research and observation of similar material.

Figure 5.1, created by Miranda Ericsson, visually represents the information life cycle of a self-published novel.

ARE YOU READY FOR THE COMMITMENT TO SELF-PUBLISH?

Some might consider self-publishing a less grueling process than the traditional path, but quite the opposite is true; the self-publishing author takes on every role and responsibility—writing, editing, design, layout, printing, promotion, storage, and distribution. Think about those lengthy "acknowledgments" in most books, and assign many of those duties to the author. A self-published author essentially is running a small business. When considering whether or not to self-publish, a writer should ask herself if she's willing to schedule her own book tour and readings, seek speaking engagements, create a Web page or pay someone to do so, and solicit reviews. The process involves much more than just uploading a manuscript and waiting for the dough and the accolades to roll in.

When planning book promotion, an author should consider any potential conflicts between his day job and public persona in the community. An elected official offering speaking engagements on her novel depicting a dystopian future, a schoolteacher signing the covers of his newly released bodice-ripper romance, or a bank employee selling a guide to getting rich may all face challenges locally from their second career as a writer.

Authors should consider hiring experienced professionals for parts of the self-publishing process because doing so may be more efficient than facing a steep learning curve to do everything well. Self-publishing means assuming all of the roles of an entire industry, including human resources and personnel management. An author must consider what skills he possesses and what tasks he might want to hire a specialist to perform. However, if an author plans to write a series, or to make a living from writing and self-publishing, then the time invested in learning all aspects of self-publishing may be rewarding. Once a person gains experience in the skills required for self-publishing, she may find that she can market her skills as services to fellow writers. Since these are emerging service industries toward self-publishing writers, this newfound expertise may find niche marketability.

In addition to evaluating her own skills, a self-published author must also evaluate the skills of others. How will she hire a high-quality, trustworthy, and experienced professional who will be a good fit for a particular project? A talented graphic designer who has never designed a book cover, a technical writer who doesn't enjoy fiction as a copyeditor, a marketing professional who doesn't know the local market for a local-interest book—all of these contributors could be the best in their field but a highly unsatisfactory choice for a specific self-publishing project.

WRITING AND EDITING

Writing is easy compared to what comes next. Programs like National Novel Writing Month (NaNoWriMo) can help writers get a first draft of a novel in 30 days, but revising and editing should take months and may take longer. Because it is possible to send a manuscript to a printer or online publisher minutes after typing the phrase "The End" doesn't mean that a writer should.

Edit. Edit. Edit . . . also, edit! There is a stereotype of self-published books as sloppy and full of errors. Don't reinforce it!

Poet and editor Leah Sewell is the founder of the Topeka Writers Workshop. She advises writers to step outside themselves as they evaluate their own work:

> I suggest that the person try to distance themselves as much as they can from the writing, both time-wise and personality-wise. Put the writing away for a week, then return to it with fresh eyes. Try donning a persona—imagine coming across the work in the pages of a literary magazine, or put yourself in the position of a blue-collar worker at a laundromat who stumbled across the magazine and flipped it open to a short story. Try to see the work from new angles, and isolate any place in the story where you, yourself, whether consciously or unconsciously, are providing the explanation. Literary work should stand on its own without further explanation. (Leah Sewell, e-mail message to author, September 2, 2015)

Workshop with other writers to gain feedback, then revise. Then workshop again, and revise again. Working with a community of writers when revising gives a writer access to more than just additional pairs of eyes seeking misplaced commas. The perspectives of beta readers and peer editors is crucial to improve a book and make it more accessible to readers who don't share the writer's unique combination of experiences and language. Another benefit of workshopping or an editing collective is the additional experience in editing and reading with a critical eye that all participants gain from reviewing other writers' work. Sharing work with a group also creates an expectation of progress and a feeling of accountability to the group, which can drive the writer to follow through and get the work done.

Sewell reminds writers to be kind to each other when workshopping. "Begin with what's working, and then move gently into revision suggestions. Read carefully, and remember the Golden Rule—treat other writers as you'd want to be treated."

> ### Leah Sewell's Questions to Consider during a Critique
>
> - Enhancements—what's good, and how can it be better?
> - Clarity—what is being expressed, and is it coming across clearly?
> - Syntax—does it flow? Is there verb-noun agreement? Is there any part of the text that tripped you up?
> - What did you see? Imagery is vital to a successful piece. What did the reader see in their mind's eye as they read? Was there anything that was difficult to imagine?

Traditionally published authors often credit the trusted members of their writing community who helped them produce better work. If needed, hire beta readers instead of skipping peer review completely.

When the writer is satisfied with the content of the manuscript, the focus shifts to copyediting. Seriously consider hiring a professional editor. Invest a bit of money for a huge payoff. Readers are turned off by typos, even when the story is good. Tiny typographical mistaks distract from the reading—and anything that takes readers from the magic of the story, the beauty of the words, or the power of the facts must be defeated. The typo in the preceding sentence is intentional, to draw attention to the jarring effect of spotting it. Online reviews of self-published books will often mention if the reader noticed typos.

Unfortunately, immaculate copyediting and proofreading is a standard by which self-published books are judged. In a traditionally published book, readers may notice a typo and tell themselves, "Oh, the poor overworked copyediting intern at a busy publishing company missed that" or make excuses like, "I'll bet the print layout introduced that mistake, and the author never even had a chance to correct it." Not so with self-published works, in which the quality control of the entire publishing process is on the shoulders of a single human.

SELECTING A PLATFORM

Once a manuscript is tightly revised, with line-by-line copyediting completed, the next step is choosing a platform for producing physical copies of the work. The author is not really choosing a publisher, since the author is the publisher, but there is still a need to pay a printer for copies of the book. The good news is that companies and their services continually evolve and hopefully improve. The bad news is that rather than simply taking the next step in the self-publishing venture and letting this book provide a recommendation for an endorsed option from a specific company, the author must consider the project and the current offerings on the market and make the best decision for her specific project and budget.

In order for an author to make an informed decision, she should think about the goals for the finished book. For example, the author may just want a stack of print copies to sell locally, or she may want the book to be available as a print-on-demand title that readers can order online and have shipped to them, or download instantly as an e-book. The author must do her homework and investigate distribution options before choosing. Also consider the reach of the platform—how should it be marketed and distributed? Are sales figures available? How do those numbers compare to similar platforms?

Whatever platform an author selects, it is important to check the terms carefully and determine what share or percentage of the sale the printer expects, what the cost per book will be for the owner ordering directly, and what restrictions apply. Read all terms and agreements carefully to make sure that exclusive agreements will not prevent the work's distribution from another platform. Simply taking advice from a fellow author isn't enough to make an informed decision for a new project. If the initial outlay of money for printing is not the sole concern, then consider these other elements in choosing a platform for publishing. This book does not endorse a particular platform and strongly recommends instead that any author preparing to self-publish consider an overall business plan when choosing a platform.

The Key Book Publishing Paths Version 2 by Jane Friedman summarizes in a single infographic what might take an entire chapter to describe in narrative text. This is a highly recommended tool for study and comparison of publishing models (https://janefriedman.com /key-book-publishing-path).

PRINTING OPTIONS

Make sure that you check out work published by the printer of your choice if at all possible. How's the quality of paper, type, cover? Does your book include illustrations or photos? A big part of the initial judgment of printed book quality is made on the quality of the print job itself. For example, a book that is not bound well or one that has streaky print stands out in a bad way. Readers may assume that the poor quality of the printing reflects poor writing and may not take the time to read the book and learn differently. Authors must make a great first impression to capture readers.

To determine the answers to some of these product quality questions, an author may need to upload a manuscript and order a proof copy from the printer. Ordering proof copies offers other advantages, too. An author can order several to share with beta readers who can help by giving a final round of feedback and catching typos. If readers enjoy the book, they may be willing to write a review in advance of the release.

Some print-on-demand facilities offer on-site printing through an Espresso Machine, which allows the printed trade paperback to be printed and bound in full view of the publisher or author (On Demand Books 2015). This device offers another avenue for authors to make their work available to customers, as titles can be ordered online or on-site in bookstores and libraries and can be printed for the customer in minutes. The novelty of seeing a book come off the presses, so to speak, is certainly memorable and would be an excellent opportunity for social media publicity about the experience.

E-BOOKS VERSUS PRINT

When an author prepares her work for publication as an e-book, formatting the manuscript so that it looks to readers just like every other e-book they are reading on their device is the priority, even though it may mean multiple edits and reformatting for the publisher. Smashwords (2015) offers a free e-book that guides authors through the process of removing the print layout formatting and preparing a manuscript to be formatted as an e-book. The

Smashwords "meatgrinder" takes the minimally formatted manuscript and creates the files for each different digital specification so that a single version can be prepared automatically for all of the current formats and give each reader on a different device a smooth reading experience. Smashwords also offers yet another avenue for authors to make their work available for sale online, as authors who use the Smashwords meatgrinder have the option to upload their work for sale through the Smashwords catalog.

E-books are a great way to increase the accessibility of an author's book. Many readers have disabilities or travel limitations that make it difficult for them to access or read printed books. Devices with assistive technology make it possible for readers with visual limitations or impairments to utilize options for text-to-speech reading, voice-guided menu navigation, adjustable font sizes, customizable screen contrast, and more. When choosing a platform for publishing an e-book, an author should see which formats would result from the process. Open format e-texts such as EPUB and Digital Accessible Information System (DAISY) are more accessible than proprietary formats such as Mobipocket (MOBI), AZW, and even PDF (Junus 2012).

Other Considerations When Self-Publishing

Draft a Sales Strategy
- First book in the series for free
- Offer excerpts online or include them in other books
- Limited time sales and discounted prices
- Integration with Goodreads consumer book review Web sites
- Integration with Amazon and other book sales Web sites
- Integration with Kindle, iBooks, and other e-book sales Web sites

Plan Financials
- Recordkeeping for filing taxes
- Budget for editing, cover art, printing, marketing
- Forming an LLC

Marketing
- Forming a small publishing press
- Business Web site
- Check criteria for inclusion in libraries and regional author fairs

---

DESIGN OR FORMATTING

Be willing to spend some money on art. A cover that attracts attention can make a huge difference! It's the first thing that most readers will notice, and it has to be good. Great book jacket artwork is about more than how the book looks in a stack at a book signing. Compare cover art on other print books in the genre at a library or bookstore. Consider how cover art may appear as a tiny thumbnail image when a reader is browsing books for sale on a phone or device.

When designing a book, compare cover details of other books—blurbs and quotes on the front or back cover, author photos and bios. Look at end matter such as excerpts and advertisements for other books, book discussion questions, and author's notes on research. Study the genre, prioritize, and don't try to include all of the ideas.

LAYOUT

A manuscript in a word processing document isn't the same as a print-ready manuscript that is sent to the printer. Layout requirements will vary depending on which service an author chooses to print a project. Currently with CreateSpace, for instance, an author can use freely provided Microsoft Word templates to create the page layout for a book, submit the files online, and digitally proof, request printed proof copies, and approve, all from standard computer software (Microsoft Office and a Web browser) available at most libraries. Some writers will want to hire a book designer to create a professional or artistic look for their layout. All self-published writers should ensure that the book they are publishing looks similar to those already on library and bookstore shelves, including the cover dimensions, front matter and end matter, text font, text size, text block size, and margins. Study other books to determine which design elements are important for a particular type of book.

DISTRIBUTING AND MARKETING

Self-published authors are their own marketing team. If the author is not willing to spend as much time writing careful jacket copy and marketing material as he would spend to pitch the book to dozens of traditional publishers, self-publishing might not work out so well.

A self-published author makes her own contacts with bookstores, libraries, and book fairs. She'll also arrange readings, signings, and book tours. Marketing means online work, and an author needs a Web site and social media presence to reach the wide world of readers. Books should be available to order online, and the author should be prepared to maintain a steady supply of books and to pack and ship books for customers or retailers if a print-on-demand company is not retained.

When considering author signings or events, think through what would entice people to attend and what would make them want to buy the book in print or as an e-book. Be prepared to help customers find the e-book if they prefer electronic format. Consider bookmarks or business cards as a way to remind people to follow up with an online purchase. Signings, author fairs, and comic cons that offer nothing but table space can be a disappointment for a reader. As a vendor, be prepared with a sales pitch and seek to engage readers in conversation. Authors should consider reading the industry news that complains about self-published authors to learn what *not* to do when marketing online and in person, and authors should also ask other local authors what is working for them.

> ### Before Ordering Books and Marketing, Consider:
> - Overhead/risk of printed books
> - Overhead/risk of consignment
> - Your time in author events
> - Cost versus the return of advertising

EXAMPLE OF A SELF-PUBLISHED BOOK FROM CONCEPT TO MARKETING

Each author's experience is unique, whether she chooses traditional or self-publishing for her work, and one author's path will never exactly match another's. Despite individual variations, though, common themes emerge when self-published authors discuss their experience. Writers who are considering self-publishing, as well as the librarians who aim to assist them, can learn a great deal from successful writers who have already made the journey. This section endeavors to relay the essence of the experience in the words of writers who have self-published one or more books.

An author might choose to self-publish her work for many reasons. Like many self-published authors, A. D. Trosper, author of the Dragon's Call series, cites timeline as a primary motivation. "I didn't want to spend an eternity wading through rejections from agents," Trosper said. "And even if I did get an agent, I didn't want to wait the time to find a publisher and then wait again for them to get around to actually putting it out there" (A. D. Trosper, e-mail message to the author, September 7, 2015).

She makes a solid point. Traditional publishing is a slow process, and it often takes several years for a book to move from acceptance to publication. For an author who is writing on a timely subject, or an author who knows that patience is not her virtue, self-publishing offers an opportunity to bypass many of the hoops that traditional authors must jump through to reach their goals.

Author Jack Campbell Jr. decided to self-publish his collection of short stories because few traditional publishers are interested in short story collections by authors who have not yet published a novel. "Collections, in general, are seen by traditional publishing as lesser endeavors," said Campbell. "They see them as promotional material and not much else" (Jack Campbell Jr., e-mail message to the author, September 6, 2015).

Campbell saw more value in short fiction than many publishers do and did not want to see his collection treated as a subpar form of writing:

> In my early days as a writer, I idolized writers who excelled at the short form. Taking the advice of Ray Bradbury's *Zen in the Art of Writing*, I learned to write by writing short stories. After several years and a lot of short story sales, I had a sufficient number of high-quality short stories for a collection. I wanted the book to be my calling card to the horror world. I wanted it to simultaneously be my informal dissertation on the genre and a symbol of my entry into literary society. I wanted to cover a large amount of ground in the collection with every type of dark fiction that I could manage. It needed to be professionally done, and I worried that the publishers who would take a diverse collection from a relatively unknown writer wouldn't be able to do it any better than I could do it myself, and that they wouldn't give it the sort of attention that I could give. (Jack Campbell Jr., e-mail message to the author, September 6, 2015)

Campbell touches on another reason that many authors choose self-publishing—control. In traditional publishing, authors relinquish control of many project details by signing a contract. The publisher may solicit the writer's opinion or work with her to achieve the writer's goals, but decisions on layout, art, and cover copy are often out of the author's hands.

A. D. Trosper also mentions control over her project as a motivating factor. "I wanted more control over the content, the cover, the price, everything. I want to have the final say in everything," Trosper said. "I had no intention of handing over all of my rights and getting paid a tiny fraction of what my books could potentially bring in" (A. D. Trosper, e-mail message to the author, September 7, 2015).

Tracy Edingfield Dunn agrees:

You can't decide whether Chapter 3 remains intact—it could be omitted, entirely, over your strenuous objections. You don't select the artwork for your cover or the title of your book. You don't get to determine who will read it and provide a "blurb" or recommendation on the flap jacket. As a writer, you're giving up a great deal, for frankly, something that isn't worth the small advance you might receive. (Tracy Edingfield Dunn, e-mail message to the author, September 7, 2015)

Author Dennis E. Smirl notes that with self-publishing, there is no bottom line or recovery of investment to deter the publication of a book:

Self-publishing is a way to get books to the public in numbers that would not work for traditional publishers. If I write a book and it sells 1,500 copies, I'm really happy. A traditional publisher would not make money on that book. If I write a book and it sells 50 copies, I'm still happy. People are reading that book. (Dennis E. Smirl, e-mail message to the author, September 1, 2015)

Aimee L. Gross mentioned that technology has legitimized self-publishing, and that the profit margin is immensely higher for self-published authors. "Self-publishing has evolved from the generally disdained 'vanity press' model to truly independent options for authors, and all over the space of a few years. Royalties of 35–70 percent, compared to 3.5–7 percent for traditionally-published authors under contract, made the new way even more attractive" (Aimee L. Gross, e-mail message to the author, October 18, 2015).

After an author chooses self-publishing, the next step is preparing a manuscript that's ready to release to the world. Successful authors recommend a thorough editing process, as described in this chapter. A. D. Trosper has her formula perfected:

I do multiple levels of editing on my books. Once I am finished with revisions on my MS, I go through it on the computer and apply any corrections I see need to be made. Then I print it out and read it out loud, marking it up as I go. Then I read it silently like I would any book, finding more things to correct. After that it goes out to several beta readers. Once I get their comments back, I fix what needs to be fixed. I do one more once over and then it goes off to my editor who marks it up even more than I did and finds everything I missed. Once I get the corrections and send them back and receive the corrected file, I load it into my Kindle and read it again. This lets me find anything that was missed while making corrections. (e-mail message to the author, September 7, 2015)

Trosper highly recommends hiring an editor:

Choose someone not related to you that is willing to put in the work. I know it costs and it can be difficult to gather the money, but it would be the same as trying to drive your car without tires because you couldn't afford them. Some things just have to be done. (e-mail message to the author, September 7, 2015)

Once the manuscript is ready, it's time to choose a printer. CreateSpace and Smashwords are popular choices for authors choosing to self-publish for the first time. Tracy Edingfield Dunn notes that Mark Coker, the founder of Smashwords, is an author himself and is sincerely motivated by helping authors' voices be heard. She's received great customer service, too.

"Whenever I have a question, I send an inquiring e-mail and get a prompt response from Smashwords that fully answers it," Dunn said. "They're genuinely interested in helping you out and are very competent in their jobs. I love that support" (Tracy Edingfield Dunn, e-mail message to the author, September 7, 2015).

CreateSpace has the advantage of linkage to Amazon, which is the largest online distributor of books in the world, and CreateSpace templates help guide authors through all of the steps of the layout process. Suzanne Dome found the process to be perfect for a first-time publisher. "I immediately liked how much control I had over the editing, formatting, and cover creation" (Suzanne Dome, e-mail message to the author, September 6, 2015).

Reaona Hemmingway originally chose CreateSpace because of a promotion that offered a free proof to NaNoWriMo winners in 2008. She's been using it ever since. "I have stayed with using them because it's easy to use, my books go up for sale on Amazon.com, and my books are available through other online booksellers. They also have distribution through Ingram's, so libraries and book stores can purchase them" (Reaona Hemmingway, e-mail message to the author, October 18, 2015).

After an author has successfully uploaded a manuscript and it has met the requirements of the chosen printer, it's time to get the book onto readers' devices or into their hands, and that means marketing. Social media, personal appearances, and reviews are a crucial part of selling a book. And for most authors, sales matter.

Brian W. Allen, who penned a memoir of his coming-of-age in the Panama Canal Zone, reminds authors, "A book that isn't sold is a story that isn't told" (Brian W. Allen, e-mail message to the author, October 20, 2015). Allen began marketing his book before he had completed the publishing process:

> I was advised by my professor to create some "buzz" for my book before publishing. He thought it would aid in marketing it to agents and help sales. I fashioned excerpts into short stories and managed to have several published in literary journals and quarterlies that interested my readers. My book was set in the Panama Canal Zone, so I accessed that population through their newsletters and on Facebook. By establishing myself as an authority, I was invited to a national reunion as a speaker and vendor. It worked very well because I knew my readership and how to access them. (Brian W. Allen, e-mail message to the author, October 20, 2015)

Poet Annette Billings notes the importance of readings to connect with audiences. "The more ways in which a potential reader can experience poetry, the more likely they are to buy. So the hearing of poetry allows for another sense to be used in addition to the eyes" (Annette Billings, e-mail message to the author, October 20, 2015).

Billings also stresses the importance of utilizing social media to connect with readers online:

Facebook has been a marvelous avenue to reach readers, and I recommend a separate Facebook page for your book(s). My sales strategy is "please," "thank you" and "would you consider?" It's very basic, but being cordial/polite and inquisitive is effective and low cost. I think my strategy has worked well for me considering the number and types of events I've been asked to do. (Annette Billings, e-mail message to the author, October 20, 2015)

Aimee L. Gross suggests that using social media is a great way to make yourself available to your readers. "I have a Facebook author page and a Twitter account, and while difficult to quantify the sales this might generate, hearing from readers who enjoyed my book is a tremendous thrill" (Aimee L. Gross, e-mail message to the author, October 18, 2015).

It's also a way to encourage reader reviews. "When a reader contacts me directly to say how much they enjoyed *If Crows Know Best*, I ask them to consider putting a review on Amazon or Goodreads," Gross said. "Most are happy to do so, and this keeps the book higher on the list in the site algorithms" (Aimee L. Gross, e-mail message to the author, October 18, 2015).

A growing number of established authors are launching self-publishing projects, too. R. L. Naquin refers to herself as a hybrid author because she publishes work through a publisher and through self-publishing:

I sold my first series, Monster Haven, to Carina Press, a digital-first imprint of Harlequin (which has since been acquired by HarperCollins). I was able to build a fan base with their help, learned how publishing works, and received more personal care with them than I might have had working directly with either Harlequin or HarperCollins. I had a great experience with Carina and have no intention of leaving them. I think combining self-publishing with traditional makes for a stronger career, at least in my case. My publisher has a broader reach than I do and can keep my name where new readers can see it, in places I can't get to by myself. (R. L. Naquin, e-mail message to the author, October 26, 2015)

Naquin notes that her two publishing paths support each other. "The two fit well together. Readers don't usually care who the publisher is. Each new release, whether it goes through a publisher or I do it myself, brings in new readers who then check out what else I've written. They funnel sales to each other" (R. L. Naquin, e-mail message to the author, October 26, 2015).

Naquin began practicing her self-publishing skills by publishing short stories that featured the characters from her Monster Haven series:

I started self-publishing slowly, experimenting with a few short stories first. For those, I kept it simple, publishing in digital format only, through Amazon Kindle Direct and with Smashwords to reach all the other vendors. The shorts were practice to learn how to format properly, learn the uploading process, figure out how to categorize and choose keywords and, later down the line, learn how to make them permanently free on Amazon, which is kind of a process all on its own. (R. L. Naquin, e-mail message to the author, October 26, 2015)

Naquin advises authors who self-publish to be adaptable and willing to try new ideas. "Self-publishing is all about the ability to be flexible and experiment. If something doesn't work, I'll do it differently the next time" (R. L. Naquin, e-mail message to the author, October 26, 2015).

New York Times bestselling author Eileen Goudge reports that for her, it was "self-publish or perish" (McCartney 2014). She published her first book in 1989 and spent years touring and receiving six-figure advances. In 2008, a recession hit and digital publishing began to seriously impact the publishing industry. Her advances withered and sales declined. Self-publishing was a way to revive her sales and keep her career as an author alive.

ADVICE FOR SELF-PUBLISHING WRITERS

To reiterate—self-publishing is a lot of work, but the payoff can be tremendous, and it is accessible and doable. Don't take it lightly. Do the research; be ready to invest time and money for a good return.

It is possible that even a fabulous book with perfect marketing and beautiful editing will fail to catch on. In the book industry, editors reject the opportunity to publish many wonderful books because they don't think they are marketable at the moment. Self-published authors have to make the decision to gamble on the market on their own, and they won't always judge the market successfully.

Self-publishing success stories vary because the measure of success is not the same for every author. For a micropublishing or niche project, a fine-quality work that advances a group's research or shares grandma's recipes with the next generation could certainly be counted a success, with no consideration of sales.

However, the most obvious triumphs are books that were originally self-published and scored a traditional contract and widespread readership, such as *The Martian* by Andy Weir (2014). Being "picked up" by a publisher still legitimizes a book and makes it official in a way that Kindle sales don't. One reason is the tradition itself; being purchased by Penguin or HarperCollins is a stamp of quality that reassures readers. Another reason is that there is a well-oiled publishing machine already in place. Writers want to be read, and traditional publishers have the framework in place to get the attention of readers and put books into libraries and bookstores all over the world.

No doubt, self-publishing authors have greater means to compete for readers than ever before, which means that the odds will continue to increase for self-published writers. A library can be a hub for local writers, a place to gather for programming and workshops and to form a network of support. Libraries can help boost local authors by providing training in the craft of writing and the technology of self-publishing, and by hosting readings and signing events for area authors. See Chapter 7 for examples from the Topeka and Shawnee County Public Library model.

CHAPTER SUMMARY

No one can truthfully say that self-publishing is easy, but advances in digital technology and communication have made publication, marketing, and distribution more accessible to independently published authors than ever before. After exploration of the current and emerging options for authors, the steps to self-publishing should be attainable to anyone committed to taking on the many roles of publisher for their manuscript.

Self-publishing is often equated with poor-quality work and is seen as a last resort for authors who are unable to publish their work through traditional channels, but that stigma is being challenged by highly successful work published independently and marketed directly to readers.

Librarians are perfectly positioned to guide and support writers in their communities as they seek information and make important decisions about publishing their work in this uncertain landscape. Partnering with writers to give them the skills to sort through the myriad of services and avenues for self-publication is an extension of reference services to the writers in their communities, and it also empowers librarians. Seeking the most accurate information and comparing potential routes for self-publishing is a perfect way to gain the insight necessary to stay current and contribute knowledgeably to the professional discussion on self-publishing.

As librarians determine the best way to adapt library services and thrive in the midst of this chaotic information age, they have an opportunity to help support the changes and craft solutions that will work for everyone involved.

REFERENCES

Coker, Mark. 2014. "2015 Book Publishing Industry Predictions: Slow Growth Presents Challenges and Opportunities." *Smashwords Blog,* December 31. http://blog.smashwords.com /2014/12/2015-book-publishing-industry.html.

Fitzgerald, Jamie. 2013. "Notable Moments in Self-Publishing History: A Timeline." *Poets & Writers,* November/December. http://www.pw.org/content/notable_moments_in_selfpublishing _history_a_timeline.

Friedman, Jane. 2013. "4 Key Book Publishing Paths: Version 2." November 19. https:// janefriedman.com/infographic-key-book-publishing-paths/

Grant, Gavin. 2015. Small Beer Press. http://smallbeerpress.com. Accessed December 2, 2015.

International Data Corporation. 2015. "Worldwide Smartphone Growth Expected to Slow to 10.4% in 2015, Down from 27.5% Growth in 2014, According to IDC." August 25. http:// www.idc.com/getdoc.jsp?containerId=prUS25860315.

Junus, S. G. Ranti. 2012. "E-books and E-readers for Users with Print Disabilities." *Library Technology Reports* 48 (7): 22–28.

McCartney, Jennifer. 2014. "How a Bestselling Author Revived Her Career by Self-Publishing." *Publishers Weekly,* October 10. http://www.publishersweekly.com/pw/by-topic/authors /pw-select/article/63962-self-publish-or-perish.html.

On Demand Books. 2015. Espresso Book Machine. http://ondemandbooks.com.

Smashwords. 2015. https://www.smashwords.com.

Weir, Andy. 2014. *The Martian.* New York: Crown.

6

LIBRARY SERVICES THAT SUPPORT WRITERS

CHAPTER OVERVIEW

Libraries serve as centers for assisting writers wishing to publish their own works. This chapter describes and illustrates activities and information resources that will assist writers striving to publish, helping authors thrive in today's ever-changing, uncertain world. Librarians and writers can form a partnership to create, organize, publish, and market their publications.

SUPPORTING LOCAL AUTHORS

The purpose of libraries is to provide cultural, recreational, educational, informational, and research resources for a community. Writers create works to raise awareness, entertain, and enlighten on a variety of topics, employing various genres—novels, nonfiction, drama, and poetry. Regardless of a writer's genre, libraries can assist authors with an assortment of print and digital resources.

Traditionally libraries have provided space for aspiring authors to assemble for book discussions and writing activities. Beyond providing meeting rooms, libraries host space in their newsletters and on their Web sites to advertise calendar events and welcome participation. Writers have an opportunity to meet face-to-face in addition to blogging or engaging in social media to exchange ideas. Authors and other clientele rely on libraries for resources, computers, and referrals to experts who can direct them on their journey. Libraries have been respected as a safe haven, providing a place for freedom of expression in a reading corner, meeting room, computer lab, or cafeteria. In recent years, libraries of all types have become more engaged in the creation of information by supporting research and creativity. This upgraded model of libraries extends the range of support services available to all customers, especially budding novelists.

Some libraries have encouraged writers by providing personnel and resources as partners in the creative process of writing. These libraries assist patrons in composing, designing, and printing paper and/or electronic copies of their works for personal use or sale. In a do-it-yourself model, local authors can access programs, events, materials, resources, and equipment in libraries at little or no expense.

Writers may feel overwhelmed by publishing complexities, and librarians can streamline this process. Whether the vehicle is a discussion group, an exhibit, or workshop series, authors can exchange stories and provide support for each other. Libraries can initiate and support writer discussion clubs, bringing authors and information professionals into a research and publishing partnership. Every library has the potential for engaging with writers in the creation, recording, and dissemination of new knowledge as part of its mission in its community.

PATHFINDERS AND LIBGUIDES

Writers should be aware of pathfinders and LibGuides as tools when they are conducting research on a topic. *Merriam-Webster Dictionary* (2014) defines *pathfinder* as "a person who goes ahead of a group and finds the best way to travel through an unknown area." Information pathfinders parallel this human pathfinder definition as research guides. Pathfinders support customers by guiding them through the quagmire along the information highway with relevant details and search engines. Pathfinders are guides that can support writers as they conduct research and reduce time searching when working on their projects.

The Emporia (Kansas) High School Library (2013) has designed and posted a variety of pathfinders assisting students and educators in their information quests. By utilizing these guides, students and staff follow a trail to complete assorted information queries. Whether searching for a book, learning how to access a database, or in a practical application such as learning how to change a flat tire, users journey through itemized steps. Library Solutions was the name ascribed to the pathfinders guiding users through assorted Web pages. Navigating Google or Google Scholar may challenge some novice searchers; however, a pathfinder directs users on a clear and concise trail, providing a systematic approach. Screen shots, diagrams, and text with directional arrows assist users in their searches.

Similar to a pathfinder is a LibGuide, which is a subscription-based platform allowing the creator flexibility within a given framework for storing documents, videos, widgets, slideshows, Web pages, and various tutorials. LibGuides are sleek with visible tabs linked to content and are easily created, updated, and edited.

Organization of resources is the LibGuide's purpose for short- or long-term projects or events. The user can register for e-mail alerts as well as view related blogs and profiles. LibGuides offer a streamlined warehouse of resources as demonstrated by Sarles (2014) and Anderson-Story (2014). "LibGuides and other Web-based research guides can similarly serve as a marketing platform with an easy-to-update interface and the ability to display multiple content types, including video" (Thompsett-Scott 2014, 17).

Pathfinders and LibGuides enhance research, reduce anxiety, and welcome access to numerous resources on the information highway. These guides can be designed and updated any time, any place at the creator's convenience. Librarians can assist authors in the creation of pathfinders or LibGuides that can be used for both research and marketing strategies. Authors can design and disseminate these print or electronic documents for educational or entertainment purposes, highlighting features of their work.

WRITER SUPPORT IN SCHOOL AND PUBLIC LIBRARIES

School and public librarians can publish and disseminate information in a variety of print and electronic platforms and provide similar training for their students and patrons. The role of academic libraries is emphasized in Chapter 9.

To sample the current practices related to self-publishing in school and public libraries, we searched for examples nationwide and conducted a survey of Kansas school and public libraries. The rationale for including Kansas public schools and libraries was to feature a typical midwestern state representing conventional beliefs and values, and the engagement of librarians with their customers in creative writing activities.

Writer Support in School Libraries

Technology impacts today's K–12 education, and school librarians can introduce self-publishing to both teachers and students. With access to various devices to create, retrieve, and disseminate information, school librarians engage their students above and beyond traditional services such as book discussion groups and story time. Since the demand for teaching information literacy skills and digital citizenship has increased, librarians partner with teachers to design lesson plans, create electronic newsletters, host Web pages, and incorporate best practices in an effort to remain current.

School librarians increasingly are focused on efforts to prepare, guide, and encourage students to learn on their own and tackle their own creative projects. Working with students and encouraging their writing and self-publishing can result in skills and self-fulfilling projects that can provide students with confidence in their writing ability. Seeing their work in print can have lifelong implications.

Engagement with students and faculty in their writing and other creative activities is documented by a recent statewide survey. In January 2015, an online survey distributed to the Kansas Association of School Librarians listserv resulted in 147 responses (Ternes 2015a). The study examined how librarians serve students and teachers in a dynamic world of printed books, electronic books, and a paperless global environment.

The results documented and quantified publishing trends observed in many school libraries. Approximately half of the respondents still created traditional print newsletters, fliers, or brochures—examples of a type of self-publishing. Nearly 20 percent did so at least monthly. Participating in the trend to create digital publications, approximately 40 percent of those who responded occasionally create electronic newsletters, fliers, or brochures, and about 26 percent created these types of documents weekly or monthly.

Librarians can bring self-publishing projects to any classroom. The survey also recognized the nationwide trend of school librarians teaching in partnership with teachers. Other major trends identified were the following:

- More than 69 percent of respondents collaborate with teachers or other librarians on a daily, weekly, or monthly basis. Monthly partnering was the most prevalent response.

- Nearly 54 percent of respondents create a PowerPoint, Prezi, or Slideshare for student lessons, faculty inservice, orientation, or training.
- While only 12 percent design a LibGuide or pathfinder, more than 56 percent of those who responded electronically publish lesson plans, photos, or school-related projects daily, weekly, or monthly, demonstrating involvement in the creative process.

Survey results also revealed other activities that are related to self-publishing.

- Some libraries have adopted a "learning commons" or "makerspace" theme, shelving books by genre or rearranging shelving and furniture, enabling and encouraging students to work together writing and creating meaningful science, technology, engineering, art, and mathematics (STEAM) projects.
- Despite a stated need for additional upgraded computers and more mobile technology, the general consensus was that school librarians would produce and publish more digital documents given adequate time and tools.
- Some school librarians have supportive parent and community involvement focusing on the needs of today's digital learners. This engagement with community can be extended to include the librarian–writer partnership for both students and adults in the community.

This survey is indicative of school librarians nationwide who are reading, writing, creating, and disseminating information in a variety of formats, as they have become self-published authors. A restricted budget may have drastically reduced professional staffing and limited collection development in some communities; nonetheless, this survey suggests that school librarians continue to maximize the resources available and nurture their students.

With the guidance of librarians, students are blossoming into critical readers, creative writers, and digital learners. School librarians can team with young aspiring artists and writers by displaying their work in the library, in their newsletters, on their Web pages, and at local events. An example of a partnership between a school and public library is the Los Gatos (California) Public Library's partnership with Los Gatos High School to publish students' e-books (Staley 2015). This collaborative approach offers a motivational, winning combination.

School librarians can also collaborate with local college librarians, encouraging students to engage in conversations and to participate in creative writing competitions, poetry readings, and local talent shows. School librarians can also connect with nearby university professors, bringing college and public school students together for writing workshops, author visits, poetry slams, performances, and publication opportunities.

Writer Support in Public Libraries

Public librarians also are using new technologies to engage clientele in their efforts to use information resources and to assist customers in their self-publishing efforts. A survey of Kansas public librarians revealed an array of technology, services, and resources (Ternes 2015b). In January 2015, an online survey distributed to the Kansas Library Association listserv for public, private, academic, college, and university librarians resulted in 126 respondents. Following are the major findings related to publishing activities:

- A significant percentage (more than 65 percent) of the respondents create a traditional printed newsletter, flier, or brochure at least quarterly. It should be noted that nearly 32 percent of the total do so monthly.
- More than 32 percent publish an electronic newsletter, flier, or brochure.
- More than 70 percent of the members who responded indicated they collaborate with educators, community members, or other librarians on a quarterly basis. Nearly 50 percent communicate monthly or weekly.
- More than 36 percent indicated they create a PowerPoint or similar presentation for orientation or training purposes on a quarterly, monthly, or weekly basis.
- Although only 32 percent of the respondents have created a LibGuide or pathfinder, nearly 46 percent of the respondents electronically publish photos, projects, or programs of events on a weekly basis. More than 80 percent do so on a monthly basis.

These responses suggest public librarians are making an effort to utilize a variety of digital technologies and social media connections in their work with customers—activities that can lead to self-publishing assistance. Although few participants design LibGuides or pathfinders, a majority of librarians publish newsletters or brochures. Libraries with limited funds for increased space, technology, professional development, and customer service have developed makerspaces and have extended creative expression into their events. Examples of partnerships can be found in which librarians team with local authors, musicians, entertainers, engineers, artists, firefighters, biologists, and business professionals, demonstrating collaboration with various community leaders and professionals.

Whether preparing a LibGuide, pathfinder, newsletter, or brochure in paper or digital format, librarians can help writers focus on their content, purpose, style, citations, and the entire publishing process. Librarians like Heather Braum (2015) have practiced for years the value of virtual libraries, where patrons access materials guided by a librarian in person, via a webinar, phone, chat, e-mail or digital conversation.

The survey participants reported a sense of eagerness to learn, collaborate, and engage in professional training. This desire to promote customer-centered services is widespread in the library profession, and the engagement of librarians with writers of all ages is a future direction for the library profession.

TRENDS IN WRITER SUPPORT SERVICES

An increasing number of libraries are providing writer support services. Here are a few representative examples.

Johnson County (Kansas) Public Libraries (JCPL) encourage teen participation in Elementia, a collection of young adult original fiction, nonfiction, poetry, graphic stories, art, and photography. The JCPL (2014) makerspace movement incorporates publishing programs serving the Kansas City area.

The Topeka Shawnee County (Kansas) Public Library (2015) boasts author visits and a writer's workshop. The Community Novel Project balances the expertise of previous participants while welcoming new writers. The library's extensive author support program is described in Chapter 7.

Writers in the Schools, a program sponsored by Seattle Arts and Lectures (2015), places professional writers in Seattle-area schools to support and encourage writing and the performance arts. Youth develop their talents through chapbooks, letters, songs, and poetry, enhancing unity in the community.

School librarians can increase collaborative efforts with academic and public librarians to promote local publishing. Celebrations of the birthday of Dr. Seuss on Read across America Day and Digital Learning Day are examples of opportunities to raise awareness about reading, writing, and publishing.

In a do-it-yourself era, library customers can access tools, resources, encouragement, and expertise at libraries at little or no expense. Whether the vehicle is a discussion group or a workshop, information users can appreciate the hands-on features of today's libraries, including various resources, extended hours, and face-to-face dialogue, in addition to phone and online chat reference support. Librarians proactively engage in conversations with patrons of all ages to partner in creative writing and publishing.

MAKING CONNECTIONS WITH SMORE

Many of us recall enjoying s'mores, roasted marshmallows and a chocolate bar sandwiched between two graham crackers at a campfire, and we may appreciate this digital version of Smore. A Web-based application for public or private newsletters, publications, fliers, and announcements, Smore (2014) connects a direct line of communication customized for the intended audience. Videos, buttons, photos, and links can be embedded in a communication.

Most features are free, and subscriptions are available at reasonable rates. Insert creative flair when designing unique digital fliers tailored for the readers. If the purpose is to inform, enlighten, or entertain, Smore offers electronic distribution. This electronic platform provides a variety of features including snapshots, statistics, charts, images, and text.

Amy Brownlee's (2014) Sterling High School *Library Connections* is published using Smore. Brownlee appreciates how the graphics look polished and professional. The text, graphics, and links are versatile. Data (analytics) recording how many views the document has received and displaying a map illustrating where the views were located are unique features. Brownlee designs and disseminates her Smore Web fliers to students, educators, parents, and community members. "It's also easy to share and can even be embedded in another page. I embedded the Smore in our library blog and created a newsletter link from our library Web page," Brownlee said.

Hailing from Mission Valley, Kansas, Rose Niland (2015) selected Smore for her school library newsletter because of its ready-made format and seasonal backgrounds. This free service is perfect for her limited budget and is appropriate for her students, faculty, staff, parents, alumni, and friends. Her newsletter inspires academic and recreational reading and student involvement, and supports learning across the curriculum.

Smore has been utilized at one of the authors' library to welcome and inform new and returning teachers and students about programs, operations, and procedures. This newsletter, *Media Matters* (2015), replaces a Word or Publisher document and articulates curricular crosswalks, promotes events, and supports literacy. Videos capturing students and staff expressing themselves can be embedded, promoting various themes and creating student connections.

The Kansas Association of School Librarians (2014) has incorporated Smore as a monthly messenger and also uses it to announce contests and awards.

A presentation by Kristina A. Holzweiss (2013) at an American Association of School Librarians conference demonstrates Smore's flexibility with clear and concise digital features in an easy-to-use interface.

Writers can use Smore Web fliers to update their readers and promote their books. Librarians can help authors promote their works economically and with a wealth of options.

BUSINESS CARDS, NEWSLETTERS, AND PUBLICATIONS

Clever business cards, bookmarks, and postcards can be designed and dispersed, providing details and promoting events that can assist authors who publish their own works. By marketing their services via social media, librarians can catch the attention of current and new writers, raising awareness about available services. Software packages provide abundant publicizing opportunities with a variety of templates and features. Enhanced business cards, stationery, and letterhead elements assist writers promoting their work. Whether in traditional paper or electronic format, sharing contact information is essential in meeting potential readers and buyers.

MailChimp (2015) and Constant Contact (2015) offer free and payment options for automating and personalizing e-mail and targeting appropriate audiences. These e-mail solutions communicate effectively and attract the attention of the intended audience.

Librarians and writers can promote their publications by designing e-mail newsletters with Email Template for Newsletters (2013). Writers can browse, create, and export fact sheets, advertisements, or inspirational messages with several prepared guides. When authors promote their works using these creative digital devices, they increase the opportunity to connect with and expand their audience.

CREATIVE PRESENTATIONS

Enhance a book talk, author event, or program by publishing an electronic slide show. Power-Point (2016) is a Microsoft Office product widely used for producing slide presentations. Prezi (2015) provides free software packages for making slide presentations. Both PowerPoint and Prezi are commonly used, user-friendly presentation templates. Since Prezi is cloud-based, more than one person can contribute to a dynamic production. Oldham (2012) presents a sample Prezi presentation. Google Slides (2015) is another free source that supports presentations with text accompanied by charts, timelines, still pictures, and videos.

Historically a popular video presentation tool, Animoto (2015) offers slides and video at free or reasonable subscription fees. Once a slide show with text, clip art, and music, Animoto has transformed into an engaging video production software package. Writers who wish to promote their works, provide biographical and historical details, or provide book references may subscribe to this service.

An information highway presentation comprising research practices, trends, and linguistic examples for improving communication can be sampled at https://animoto.com /play/iriN0peoYzyFFA2VMbHkxQ in a literate librarian animoto capturing numerous common library practices. Another example from a middle school librarian captures the essence of orientation (http://crossroadssouthlibrary.pbworks.com/w/page/44587781/Library%20Orientation).

Christy Yacano's animoto presents photos capturing her students in a "So much to see; so much to do @ your Library" theme demonstrating the value of a library partner. Enjoy this exemplary Colorado school librarian's message at https://animoto.com/play/cWEftEjlbOMO9Z24wJqaWg. This slide show illustrates how writers can construct their self-publishing quest.

A more recent presentation tool, PechaKucha (2015), recommends twenty images with twenty seconds dedicated to each slide in an effort to captivate viewers, using eye-catching photos, graphics, statistics, and fonts. Although the Japanese origin of the name PechaKucha means "chatter," the presentations capture the audience's attention without overwhelming photos, text, or noise. Check out examples on the PechaKucha Web site, and also be aware of Apple's Keynote (2015) presentation software.

Writers may benefit from creating an electronic presentation in order to capture a reader's interest. Since these Web-based platforms engage the reader with descriptive text, images, videos, and music, authors can effectively advertise their books via social media and ask readers and fans to share.

CHAPTER SUMMARY

Libraries traditionally have provided space for aspiring authors to assemble for book discussions and writing activities. In recent years libraries of all types have become more engaged in the creation of information by supporting research and creativity, including supporting writers who wish to self-publish.

An increasing number of libraries support writers by providing personnel and resources as partners in the creative process of writing. These libraries assist patrons in creating, designing, and disseminating paper and/or electronic copies of their works for personal use or sale.

Subscription-based and freely available Web 2.0 features can support writers with LibGuides and pathfinders as writers conduct research for their works, and these finding aids can promote authors' books. Also, librarians can partner with writers to utilize social media, publication and presentation software, and other recent developments in technology to promote self-published books.

REFERENCES

Anderson-Story, Janet. 2014. Welcome to the FHTC LibGuides Page. http://libguides.fhtc.edu/index.php. Accessed November 29, 2015.

Animoto. 2015. https://animoto.com. Accessed November 29, 2015.

Braum, Heather. 2015. Open Education Resources and the Open Web: Collaborating and Sharing for Student Success. http://www.symbaloo.com/mix/openeducationresources. Accessed March 17, 2015.

Brownlee, Amy. 2014. Library Connections. https://www.smore.com/a89gs-library-connections. Accessed February 23, 2015.

Constant Contact. 2015. Be a Marketer. http://www.constantcontact.com/index.jsp. Accessed November 28, 2015.

Email Template for Newsletters. 2013. http://www.email-newsletter-template.com. Accessed November 29, 2015.

Emporia High School Library. 2013. Library Solutions: EHS Library Catalog Pathfinder. http://www.usd253.org/home/ehslib. Accessed November 28, 2015.

Google Slides. 2015. Create Beautiful Presentations. https://www.google.com/slides/about. Accessed November 29, 2015.

Holzweiss, Kristina A. 2013. The Common Core Conversation. https://www.smore.com/gwgv. Accessed January 9, 2015.

Johnson County Public Libraries. 2014. *Elementia*. http://jocolibrary.org/teens/elementia. Accessed April 12, 2015.

Kansas Association of School Librarians. 2014. KASL Newsflyer. https://www.smore.com/b3tau-kasl. Accessed March 1, 2015.

Keynote. 2015. Keynote for Mac. http://www.apple.com/mac/keynote. Accessed November 28, 2015.

MailChimp. 2015. http://mailchimp.com/features/email-templates. Accessed August 22, 2015.

Media Matters. 2015. Media Matters Welcome 2015. https://www.smore.com/y02vj-media-matters-2014-welcome. Accessed November 28, 2015.

Merriam Webster. 2014. Pathfinder. http://www.merriam-webster.com/dictionary/pathfinder. Accessed April 29, 2015.

Niland, Rose. 2015. Mission Valley Library News. https://www.smore.com/8r4w4. Accessed February 23, 2015.

Oldham, Lisa. 2012. The Future Focused School Library.https://prezi.com/_sjom2s0g-zy/the-future-focused-school-library. Accessed November 29, 2015.

PechaKucha. 2015. http://www.pechakucha.org. Accessed June 18, 2015.

PowerPoint. 2016. https://office.live.com/start/PowerPoint.aspx. Accessed June 18, 2015.

Prezi. 2015. https://prezi.com. Accessed June 18, 2015.

Sarles, Patricia. 2014. LibGuides. http://jeromeparkercampus.libguides.com. Accessed April 29, 2015.

Seattle Arts and Lectures. 2015. Writers in the Schools. https://www.lectures.org/wits/writers_n_schools.php. Accessed June 18, 2015.

Smore. 2014. Beautiful Newsletters in Minutes. https://www.smore.com. Accessed December 12, 2014.

Staley, Lissa. 2015. "Leading Self-Publishing Efforts in Communities." *American Libraries.* 46: 18-19.

Ternes, Carmaine. 2015a. "Blossoming Successful School Libraries." Unpublished paper. Microsoft Word file.

Ternes, Carmaine. 2015b. "Forecasting the Future of Libraries—Kansas Library Association SurveyCompass." Unpublished paper. Microsoft Word file.

Thompsett-Scott, Beth, ed. 2014. *Marketing with Social Media: A Library and Information Technology Association Guide.* Chicago, IL: American Library Association.

Topeka Shawnee County Public Library. 2015. Community Novel Project. https://tscpl.org/community-novel/about. Accessed March 17, 2015.

7

THE TOPEKA AND SHAWNEE COUNTY PUBLIC LIBRARY MODEL

CHAPTER OVERVIEW

Connecting writers to one another is as core to our profession as connecting people to print or digital library resources. Libraries can support authors with resources, programming, and encouragement, and one of the most important things that libraries can provide to writers is the opportunity to connect to other writers and readers in a friendly and encouraging space. Building a community of writers and increasing access to self-publishing resources helps shift the perception of the library from a passive repository of materials to an active ally for self-published authors.

At the Topeka and Shawnee County Public Library, we connect the people of our community to one another, even as we connect them to literature, technology, and cultural enrichment. We're building a community of writers, with the library as a hub for creation and collaboration. In this chapter, librarians can learn more about the Topeka and Shawnee County Public Library model to support local writers, which started with National Novel Writing Month (NaNoWriMo) and Community Novel Project and has expanded to include other skills programming, an annual workshop, and an annual author fair.

COME WRITE IN

At our library, we can trace the genesis of community writing programs to the implementation of NaNoWriMo in the library. In October 2004, librarian Lissa Staley presented a library program to promote the library's fiction-writing resources and encourage community members to try to write novels in the thirty days of November. In successive years, the library added write-ins in the computer lab, which were Sunday afternoon events when novelists gathered to write their individual novels.

After several years of increasing participation in NaNoWriMo, customers requested programs about editing and publishing. The library responded by bringing in a professional editor and ghostwriter to offer tips and advice for writers to revise and edit their work. For writers seeking information on preparing their manuscripts for submission, the library continued to make the traditional referrals to trusted sources like *Writer's Digest*, along with local referrals to writing organizations. This limited programming allowed the library to engage new and emerging writers with information and referral, which met the need at the time and adhered to the traditional library role. In 2014, our library was featured in an *American Libraries* article about how libraries embrace NaNoWriMo programming (Morehart 2014).

This simple model could have been sustainable for years; however, the proliferation of mobile technology and readily available Wi-Fi quickly changed the publishing industry, and the demand increased from customers to learn more about self-publishing from their library.

Even when customers have the ability to write, edit, and publish their work within the library's space with the technology provided for public use, the library cannot become the personal support staff for individual creative business entities. In order to serve the growing demand from writers while staying within the bounds of feasibility, we needed to promote a model that was still open to anyone to accomplish on their own.

We continued to be challenged by how to offer programming that would be scalable and adaptable to writers of varying skill levels and at different stages in the editing and publishing process. The library doesn't focus only on novice writers, but aims to support writers throughout all stages of their writing careers.

TRYING SOMETHING NEW

How can a library create a common goal that benefits the library and also benefits writers of varying skill levels individually? When the wild idea of the library sponsoring a round-robin–style writing project was introduced in a staff meeting in early 2012, several staff members saw the opportunity to experiment with the looming questions being raised by the local writing community. A collaboratively written novel, with each writer contributing a sequential chapter, would engage many writers in a single work. By publishing the book under our auspices and providing staff as project organizers, the library positioned ourselves as a convener of local content creation and supporter of individual growth. All contributing writers were challenged to stretch outside their own comfort zone to continue the collaborative story. The end result of a published book was an accomplishment for the library, the contributing writers, and the community to celebrate.

The first year of the experiment that became the Community Novel Project has been repeated, changed, and improved annually. We work in pilot project mode, constantly seeking places to raise the bar, to let things go, and to evaluate success and opportunities for change. Rather than present a generalized model in the abstract, we offer an accounting of our experiments, including what we have learned the hard way, what we would do differently, and how these ideas may be scalable and adaptable to other libraries and other communities.

2012 COMMUNITY NOVEL PROJECT: *CAPITAL CITY CAPERS*

Figure 7.1, the book cover of *Capital City Capers,* shows artwork from the 2012 Community Novel Project.

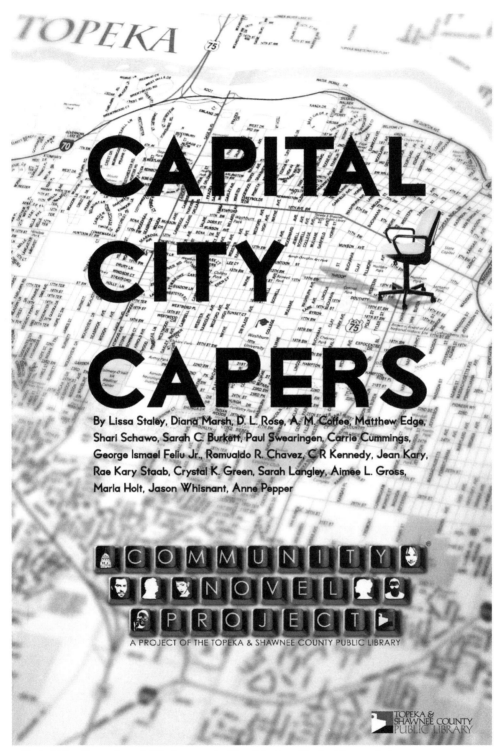

CAPITAL CITY CAPERS

By Lissa Staley, Diana Marsh, D. L. Rose, A. M. Coffee, Matthew Edge, Shari Schawo, Sarah C. Burkett, Paul Swearingen, Carrie Cummings, George Ismael Feliu Jr., Romualdo R. Chavez, C R Kennedy, Jean Kary, Rae Kary Staab, Crystal K. Green, Sarah Langley, Aimee L. Gross, Marla Holt, Jason Whisnant, Anne Pepper

COMMUNITY NOVEL PROJECT

A PROJECT OF THE TOPEKA & SHAWNEE COUNTY PUBLIC LIBRARY

TOPEKA &
SHAWNEE COUNTY
PUBLIC LIBRARY

Capital City Capers from 2012 Community Novel Project. Used with permission.

In 2012, for our first pilot project, a few librarians were given permission to explore this idea and try to bring it to fruition. The idea was first mentioned at a January 2012 meeting and within nine months we had nurtured our first completed community novel, *Capital City Capers*. To begin the pilot, the library staff created a title, premise, and first chapter of a story that they believed other members of the community could enjoy writing. The first challenge was creating an opening chapter that established the direction of the novel while leaving the story, characters, and plot open for community writers to develop and advance. The second challenge was finding the next few writers to continue the story before any element of the project had been advertised or serialized on the library's Web site. The librarians' prior participation in the writing community was crucial in convincing writers to volunteer their time and talents to a project unlike any they had seen succeed before.

Make It Your Own: Find a Champion

If your library doesn't have a staff person with writing connections, find a champion in the writing community to recruit writers to the project. In order to set the tone for cooperation rather than competition, establish your library as a convener of collaboration, with community engagement and learning as the goal rather than financial gain or fame.

Our goals for the first year were to publish a chapter each week online and publish a finished printed book in time for the Author Book Launch Party on September 30, 2012. The physical takeaway was the printed book, signed and sold at the library's book launch event and still available through Amazon's print-on-demand service CreateSpace. With a goal of making the book accessible, the minimum price point is set through CreateSpace, and no royalties are generated when the book is purchased. The library ordered copies at the discounted price available to the book's publisher and resold the book for $5 preorder and $6 at book launch.

Capital City Capers, 2012

Printed books cost $3.37 per book plus $0.43 each for shipping
$3.80 total cost to publisher; list price: $5.62 at amazon.com
Product dimensions: 8 x 5.2 x 0.5 inches, 210 pages

Our project's goals of teaching community writers the skills needed for self-publishing evolved from the steep learning curve that we faced in layout and publication for our first book. Lowering the barriers to other writers' success and using technology that was freely available from the public library became central to our planning moving forward.

A self-publishing author must leave the comfort of her writing desk to become the project manager of her publishing team. Writing the acknowledgments for the project made it obvious that supporting an interest in self-publishing was about more than helping someone develop writing skills. Specifically naming and crediting the many people who worked behind the scenes broadens awareness of the numerous professionals required to accomplish a successful self-published book: copyeditors, webmasters, graphic designers, marketing specialists, legal advisers, and financial consultants.

Engaging the local writing community in this type of published project also means letting go of some control. While previous library programs had offered encouragement and advice for writers, this new level of engagement actively placed the library and librarians in a role to evaluate and critique individual writing efforts.

In an anonymous participant survey following the book launch, writers shared feedback from their experience with the project. A recurring theme was the challenge of trying something new, or as one writer noted: "It pushed me outside my comfort zone, and honestly, I liked that" (*Capital City Capers* 2012b). A more experienced writer added: "I also enjoyed thoroughly the reactions of those writers who had never experienced having something they'd written published—watching several of them clutch the novel to their bosoms was priceless."

Appendix A includes more details from the 2012 Community Novel Project including lessons learned, software and online tools used, and task lists.

2013 COMMUNITY NOVEL PROJECT: *SPEAKEASY*

Figure 7.2, the *SpeakEasy* book cover from the 2013 Community Novel Project, features all of the authors' names.

Going into the second year of the project, we drew on the experience of the first project to identify areas for improvement and better articulate goals for participants and the library.

In 2013, more than 20 writers contributed chapters for the novel *SpeakEasy*, which was serialized on the library Web site from April to August 2013. The Web site also offered extras for readers in the community, including behind-the-scenes information on how the project was organized and interviews with the authors. The novel is still available on the original site, and it is now available as a complete edition in print, audiobook, and e-book format.

Returning community novel authors were strong contributors to the process. A big change for this project was that the premise was developed as a group, although challenges arose when unexpected plot twists were revealed early in the book. The guideline that we stress to all collaborative writers is that their chapter should build on the chapters that came before theirs, while leaving the story open to possibilities.

Make It Your Own: Organize Writers

Your project organizer must guide individual writers to stick to the plot outline. Opening chapters must accomplish different benchmarks for the story development than middle or closing chapters. Coach each consecutive writer to consider only what has already happened in the story and what his or her chapter will add. As contributing writer Diana Marsh shared, "The challenge, as with every year, is not starting to plot your chapter too soon, based on the chapters several ahead of you, because everything you've planned for might be undone in the very next chapter" (*SpeakEasy* 2013a, 164). Your project organizer leads the cohesive collaborative effort of the writers.

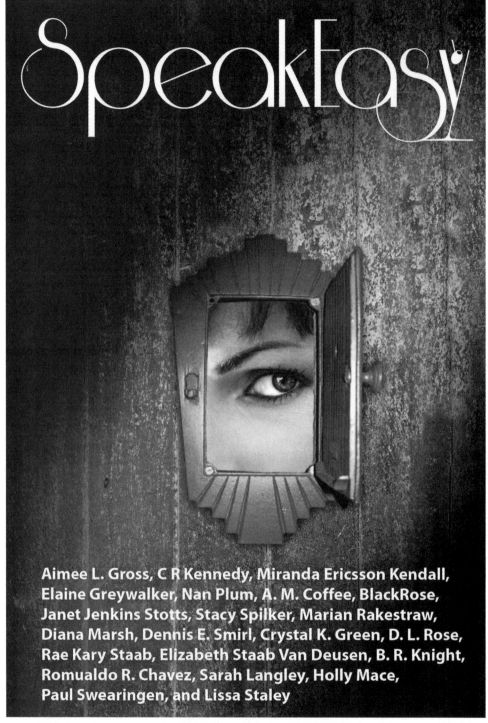

SpeakEasy

Aimee L. Gross, C R Kennedy, Miranda Ericsson Kendall,
Elaine Greywalker, Nan Plum, A. M. Coffee, BlackRose,
Janet Jenkins Stotts, Stacy Spilker, Marian Rakestraw,
Diana Marsh, Dennis E. Smirl, Crystal K. Green, D. L. Rose,
Rae Kary Staab, Elizabeth Staab Van Deusen, B. R. Knight,
Romualdo R. Chavez, Sarah Langley, Holly Mace,
Paul Swearingen, and Lissa Staley

SpeakEasy from 2013 Community Novel Project. Used with permission.

Based on the interesting stories shared by authors about their experiences at the *Capital City Capers* book launch, we decided to interview authors throughout the writing process and share the interviews alongside chapters as they were serialized online, and also to include the interviews as part of the printed book. We incorporated more peer editing through a shared wiki and designated continuity editors and copyeditors. In order to offer additional formats, we released an audiobook version with each new serialized chapter. We modeled examples of book promotion by engaging the writers in the marketing, including social media, interviews with local media, and interacting in person with potential readers.

The *SpeakEasy* e-book (2013b) is freely downloadable directly from the library's Web site in PDF, EPUB, and Mobi formats. Readers can view, download, or read online at Smashwords in multiple formats, and the book is discoverable by browsing or searching any of the contributor names.

SpeakEasy, 2013

Printed books cost $3.41 per book plus $0.42 each for shipping
$3.83 total cost to publisher; list price: $5.69 at amazon.com
Product dimensions: 9 x 6 inches, 214 pages

The author interviews from *SpeakEasy* provide insight into the value of the project for the participants. Marian Rakestraw shared: "Committing to writing a chapter for the Community Novel and knowing it would be published was a way to force myself to let other people read my work" (*SpeakEasy* 2013a, 179). Writer C R Kennedy wrote one of the early chapters in the story. She commented: "It's exciting to follow the path the story takes after it leaves your hands, and thrilling when someone down the line decides to nurture a seed that you planted, and you get to watch it grow in a way you never imagined" (*SpeakEasy* 2013a, 169). After returning to the project for a second year, writer D. L. Rose contributed a broader perspective in her statement:

> No two authors think alike. I think that's both the challenge and the beauty of collaborative writing. Two authors could look at the same premise and start it different ways. And each author would continue from what came before in a different way. It is definitely a practice in what it really means to let your writing stand on its own. If you have to explain to the next author what you were doing in your chapter, you probably weren't doing it right. (*SpeakEasy* 2013a, 190)

Appendix B includes more details from the 2013 Community Novel Project including changes made to the project with editing, continuity, audiobooks, interviews, and marketing.

2014 COMMUNITY NOVEL PROJECTS

The biggest change for this year's project was that the writing community decided to create two novels simultaneously. One project was a 20-chapter novel for adult readers, much like the first two projects. A number of writers from previous projects had expressed interest in writing for a middle-grade or young adult audience, so the second project was a ten-chapter juvenile novel that allowed those writers and others to create content for younger readers. We also planned to offer more opportunities than ever before for learning new skills, with training in Web publishing and print layout offered to interested participants.

In retrospect, this scaling up of the project quantity was in the wrong direction. Rather than doubling down on the skills training for writers and focusing twice as much effort on a single novel, we diverted our efforts into two separate projects. This example is not unfamiliar to a self-publishing author who scales up her operation instead of devoting her attention to a single title at a time. In 2014, we published two books that we are proud of—*Superimposed* and *Spirits of Oz*. *Spirits of Oz* addressed a middle-grades audience and included illustrations. *Superimposed* alternated between contemporary and historical time-lines. With three possible genres, writers had more options than in previous years to pick what they wanted to write.

To promote readership of the novels online as they were being serialized, the library's podcast, *Hush*, interviewed writers from the two community-written collaborative novels and released a special double episode. The Community Novel Project was also given a promotional boost through the honor of a Literary Arts "ARTY" award from ARTSConnect, a Topeka organization that promotes the arts and broadens understanding of how the arts enhance the quality of life in our community. ARTSConnect promoted nominees through social media with their network, potentially reaching readers that our library might not have reached. In addition to giving a great sense of pride to the individual writers, the award provided community recognition from outside of the library that our collaborative work is a significant contribution to the arts scene. These marketing efforts along with the book launch and book signing featuring dozens of writers made this two-book project year a success.

Figure 7.3, *Spirits of Oz,* targeted a middle-grades audience during the 2014 Community Novel Project.

Spirits of Oz, 2014

Printed books cost $3.34 per book plus $0.43 each for shipping
$3.77 total cost to publisher; list price: $5.57 at amazon.com
Product dimensions: 6 x 9 inches, 208 pages

Spirits of Oz challenged writers to consider the intended middle-grades audience. Writer Marian Rakestraw shared: "I wrote the chapter with the help of my children, James and Sophia. We had a wonderful time taking a field trip to the Rochester Cemetery, brainstorming all the things they wanted to include, and discussing what they thought Nico and Lola would think and say. Without their help this would be a very different chapter" (*Spirits of Oz* 2014, 148). Sky Kendall was the youngest author on this project, a 12-year-old co-writing with his uncle, but he reflected a common theme in his interview: "I can't really force my creative work, which is why it was nice to pick up where the last author left off. It gave us some inspiration" (*Spirits of Oz* 2014, 161).

Spirits of Oz from 2014 Community Novel Project. Used with permission.

> ### *Superimposed*, 2014
> Printed books cost $3.46 per book plus $0.43 each for shipping
> $3.89 total cost to publisher; list price: $5.77 at amazon.com
> Product dimensions: 6 x 9 inches, 218 pages

As the annual project continued, many authors found reasons to return. "This is my third year participating, and I keep coming back for the same reason every time—the joy and wonder of creating something, something wild and insane and fantastic, with a group of creative, inspired individuals," shared Diana Marsh (*Superimposed* 2014, 163). First-time contributor Reaona Hemmingway added: "The Community Novel Project provides a means to not only try something new like collaborating with other authors, but also an opportunity to reach a new audience with my writing" (*Superimposed* 2014, 173).

Appendix C includes more details from the 2014 Community Novel Project including plot summaries and changes to the previous process.

Illuminating the self-published fiction creation process for writers is one of the core values of this project. Reading a fiction book doesn't show you the creation process and the behind-the-scenes details. In Appendix D, we share an example from *Superimposed* to turn the abstract idea of collaborative fiction writing into interactions you can visualize.

> ### Make It Your Own: Involve the Entire Community
> Keep track of all contributors throughout the process of your library's project, whether you include everyone by name in the acknowledgments or express gratitude throughout the process. From administrators who grant permission to proceed with a pilot project to the local reporter who covers the story of the book launch, celebrate each person involved in creating a successful self-publishing experience to bring attention to the diverse roles and responsibilities in this endeavor.

2015 COMMUNITY NOVEL PROJECT: *TIME HARBOR*

After evaluating our 2014 projects, we realized that organizing two concurrent projects wasn't realistic or repeatable. We anticipated that after including more than thirty authors in the 2014 projects that demand for participation in 2015 would exceed our previous 20-chapter outline model. We have learned that many previous participants in the Community Novel Project choose to contribute to future projects, and we always want to be engaging new participants as well.

In planning the 2015 premise meeting, we looked for a way to modify the project so that we could include a variable number of participants. We settled on the idea of writing a Pick a Path story with multiple plotlines for readers to follow, modeled on the popular Choose Your Own Adventure series. This concept allowed us to be flexible in adding additional authors as the paths of the plot branched out in new directions. For the first time, instead of mapping the premise onto a generic 20-chapter outline, a contributing writer developed and diagrammed an original outline for the book's complex plot.

Make It Your Own: Delegate Opportunities to Learn

Challenge yourself not to do all the work. Encourage writers to take on more responsibility. If the goal is to model and teach self-publishing skills to interested writers, they need hands-on experience. Contributor Crystal K. Green shared, "Each time through, I gain so much insight into how to plan, write, and edit better. This year, in addition to writing a chapter, I wanted to contribute to the behind-the-scenes editing frenzy. I've spent hours proofreading, fact checking, asking questions, and creating an event timeline to help us track our characters' pasts and presents" (*Superimposed* 2014, 184).

Our 2015 programming offered events that directly benefited individual writers and raised the quality of the project. We helped writers focus on genre guidelines at the premise meeting by establishing parameters for the story in advance. Reflecting on our past experiences with uncontrolled brainstorming during collaborative premise development, we tightly facilitated the discussion to help the group reach consensus. We addressed narrative point of view and character development as skills that writers could practice and improve with this project. We used the characters and narrative voice of *Time Harbor* as examples while we discussed broader techniques that would be helpful for any fiction writer. A book layout workshop covered the terminology of book layout and detailed the steps to consider when self-publishing, in print or e-book format.

During the writing process the novel in progress was featured in a full-page article in *Library Journal*, providing publicity that any author or publisher would covet (Verma 2015b).

Appendix E further describes the 2015 project: premise guidelines and meeting agenda, in-depth program descriptions, initial story details established by the group, and a plot summary that reveals significant dates in Topeka history that are featured in the story.

Moving forward, the library is more closely integrating all programming related to writers. The community novel project has focused primarily on fiction writing, but community members have indicated interest in writing and self-publishing poetry, memoir, nonfiction, and children's books. The library will continue to engage new and established writers by focusing on lifelong learning and interacting with writers as individual business owners. While the library is a supportive resource for skills development and professional growth for writers, we're also in the business of connecting readers to books that they will enjoy. It's a natural fit that we help promote these writers' products.

Make It Your Own: Evaluate, Then Improve

Establish what success will look like for your library and your writing community. Measure traditional metrics like program attendance, book sales, checkouts, and downloads. In addition, consider evaluating success based on participation, media coverage, increased community engagement around writing, and the individual projects that authors bring to market after being part of your program. Ask your writers to provide testimonials and intentionally interview them about the process.

THE ARC OF WRITERS PROGRAMMING

Our library's annual Great Writers, Right Here author fair brings significant marketing attention to regional literary talent through diverse representation of authors. The transition to a single annual event reflects how library programming for self-published writers has changed over the last several years. Instead of trying to give each local author a small book-signing event, we focus on a single unified event to meet that purpose more efficiently and on a much grander scale. This consolidation frees staff time and calendar space for several featured author events and writing events that focus on techniques, skills, and collaboration.

Successive years of the author fair have included a more selective application process, increased social media marketing, instructive promotion techniques for participants, and featured readings from prominent local talents. Each year we aim to host a fantastic event for our reading public, while also providing an opportunity for authors to network with each other, grow professionally, sell books, and reach new readers.

Just as not every writer with a first draft after NaNoWriMo is ready to self-publish, not every self-published author is prepared to promote her book. As part of the continuum of lifelong learning programming on this topic, the library offers a morning of TED-style talks delivered by successful regional authors. Topics at this annual Local Writers Workshop span all aspects of the craft, as well as publishing and marketing for nonfiction, memoir, poetry, fiction, and graphic novels. The workshop is an opportunity to expand beyond fiction writing, which is covered heavily in programming for the Community Novel Project and NaNoWriMo.

Make It Your Own: Set Project Goals

Before you organize a writing contest, decide if your library's goal is to develop the skills of writers or to reward the best writer. When planning your library's self-publishing project, decide if the process encourages writers to support one another or compete. Before you begin a huge initiative, make connections to the existing writing communities in your region, find out what is needed, engage potential partners, and avoid duplication.

As self-publishing trends continue to change the opportunities and interests of library customers, our lifelong learning programming for writers should be responsive to community demand. Libraries have the ability to guide genealogists micropublishing their family histories, schoolchildren creating a poetry collection, or neighborhoods commemorating a significant anniversary just as easily as we can help the next bestselling authors bring their works to market.

While libraries have changed dramatically in recent years based on technology advances, the core mission of connecting people with information remains strong. Whether a library is adding a makerspace, a digital studio, focusing on self-publishing, or pursuing the next trend that comes along, staying current with emerging technologies in a lifelong learning framework positions the library as a hub for content creation in the community.

To read more about the history of this transition in programming at our library, our learning experiences with hosting a large author fair, and the details of the 2015 Local Writers Workshop, see Appendix F.

Make It Your Own: Connect Your Community to Self-Publishing

Use a Community Novel Project to highlight your library's collection of self-published books or to promote your e-book circulation model. Connect with writing programs at academic institutions and secondary schools and encourage emerging writers to self-publish anthologies, chapbooks, or zines. Invite local celebrities or renowned writers to participate and lend their notoriety to the project. Organize the project as a fundraiser, like the Stanislaus County Library in Modesto, California (Clark 2014). Solicit local history contributions or themed short stories to commemorate a significant anniversary or cultural touchstone. Demonstrate the process and the value of self-publishing to those who can benefit from the knowledge.

CHAPTER SUMMARY

Promoting self-publishing and supporting writers through library services is easier in theory than in practice. In early 2015, *American Libraries* identified libraries leading self-publishing efforts in communities as an emerging trend (Staley 2015). Serving writers through public programming creates challenges unique to each institution, because libraries vary in size, service area, funding, staffing, and service goals. Every library is unique, and the programming offered should align with the mission of the library and the needs and wants of the community. Additionally, librarians must curate quality public events while empowering emerging authors with equal access to events and resources, which can pit one core value of the profession against another. Finding the right strategy will likely be a process of trial and error, and librarians must be willing to experiment, fail, evaluate, and try again.

As part of the Community Novel Project, writers can individualize the benefit for themselves. Writers can work on dialogue, focus on writing stronger characters, or whatever they identify as skills that need improvement—and they can do it with the support of a writing community. The project is customizable to writers of all levels.

We prioritize skills building and community engagement because the foundation of our writing programming came from NaNoWriMo, which is founded on the principle that anyone can write a novel. Rather than hosting contests that create winners, losers, and competition within our writing community, we help everyone who is interested learn more about the craft of writing, self-publishing options, and the business of being a writer.

Libraries that support writers in skill development and marketing success can become the hub of a thriving writing community and an integral piece of the literary culture of their communities. It is a lot of work, but payoffs could include an engaged writing community, a greater number of successful regional authors, and a proud community of readers. This is a model that has worked for us. What works for your library may look very different. In this chapter and the appendices, we reveal the behind-the-scenes details of our community writing programs. We welcome you to visit our updated project Web site at http://www.tscpl.org/novel.

In the same way that libraries help people get jobs, help people graduate, and help kids learn to read, libraries can help people achieve their goal of being a published author. At TSCPL, we don't wave a magic wand and make people into published authors, and we don't do the work for them. We give them access to technology, resources, and research. We provide referrals to writing groups or local professionals, a community meeting space to network, and a quiet space to write. We empower writers to accomplish their own lifelong learning goals.

And we love what we do.

REFERENCES

Capital City Capers. 2012a. By Lissa Staley, Crystal K. Green, Sarah Langley, Marla Holt, Aimee L. Gross, Jason Whisnant, Diana Marsh, Anne Pepper, D. L. Rose, A. M. Coffee, Matthew Edge, Sarah C. Burkett, Shari Schawo, Paul Swearingen, George Ismael Feliu Jr., Carrie Cummings, C R Kennedy, Romualdo R. Chavez, Jean Kary, Rae Kary Staab. Topeka, KS: Topeka and Shawnee County Public Library.

Capital City Capers. 2012b. Participant Survey, September 2012.

Clark, Pat. 2014. "Stanislaus County Community Novel Launch Party Saturday," *Modesto (CA) Bee*, October 30. http://www.modbee.com/news/local/article3485248.html.

Hartman, Thad, and Lissa Staley. 2014. *Hush—New Books, Bestsellers, Literature and Reading*, podcast audio, July 11. http://traffic.libsyn.com/topekalibrary/Podcast60_Part_2.mp3.

Morehart, Phil. 2014. "A Novel in 30 Days: Libraries Embrace NaNoWriMo." *American Libraries* (November/December):19.

SpeakEasy. 2013a. By Lissa Staley, Marian Rakestraw, Diana Marsh, Dennis E. Smirl, Crystal K. Green, D. L. Rose, Rae Kary Staab, Elizabeth Staab Van Deusen, Romualdo R. Chavez, B. R. Knight, Sarah Langley, Aimee L. Gross, Holly Mace, Paul Swearingen, C R Kennedy, Miranda Ericsson Kendall, Elaine Greywalker, A. M. Coffee, BlackRose, Janet Jenkins Stotts, Stacy Spilker. Topeka, KS: Topeka and Shawnee County Public Library.

SpeakEasy. 2013b. By Lissa Staley. Smashwords, September 3. https://www.smashwords.com /books/view/353992.

Spirits of Oz. 2014. By Miranda Ericsson, Paul Swearingen, L. J. Williams, Marian Rakestraw, Aimee L. Gross, Jak Kendall, Sky Kendall, Rose Pennock, Chris Blocker, Roxanna Namey, Romualdo Chavez. Topeka, KS: Topeka and Shawnee County Public Library.

Staley, Lissa. 2015. "Leading Self-Publishing Efforts in Communities." *American Libraries* (January–February): 18–19.

Staley, Lissa, and Miranda Ericsson. 2014. "NCompass Live: Engaging Writers with a Community Novel Project." Nebraska Library Commission. https://www.youtube.com/watch?v =VNlXQYMzT_s&feature=youtu.be.

Superimposed. 2014. By Lissa Staley, George Ismael Feliu Jr., Reaona Hemmingway, Sarah Langley, Elaine Greywalker, A. M. Coffee, Diana Marsh, Stacy Spilker, Dennis E. , Elizabeth Staab Van Deusen, Miranda Ericsson Kendall, Brian W Allen, Holly Mace, Marian Rakestraw, Craig Paschang, Nora E. Derrington, Steve Laird, Crystal K. Green, Liv Howard, Annette Komma. Topeka, KS: Topeka and Shawnee County Public Library.

Verma, Henrietta. 2015a. "Engaging Your Local Writing Community." Webcast video, 62:00. Library Journal. http://lj.libraryjournal.com/2015/06/webcasts/engaging-your-local -writing-community.

Verma, Henrietta. 2015b. "It Takes a City to Create a Novel." *Library Journal* (July): 23.

SOCIAL MEDIA TO PROMOTE YOUR PUBLICATION

CHAPTER OVERVIEW

In recent years social media have entered the mainstream and can be used to promote any book or publication. Digital learners can be targeted today by effective electronic advertising strategies. Librarians can support their budding authors and other clientele with resources employing a variety of marketing principles and provide them with comprehensive instructions (Thomsett-Scott 2014).

With the proliferation of assorted cell phones, computers, and portable electronic devices, social media have become a norm in today's global society. Due to the attractiveness of technology in and beyond the workplace, consumers of all ages may experience a sense of wonderment when learning and utilizing these interactive and collaborative features. This chapter presents tools that enable librarians and writers to collaborate in order to publish and promote publications and facilitate understanding current online communities and evaluating future developments.

CREATING COLLABORATIVE COMMUNITIES

Self-publishing is best accomplished when a writer works with other writers, librarians, and people knowledgeable about publishing processes—the creation, recording, reproduction, and dissemination of information. Whenever possible, face-to-face interactions still remain a favored way to collaborate; however, newer technologies and social media allow writers and librarians to collaborate at a distance as they strive to write and self-publish. Several resources that can facilitate collaboration are presented.

Facebook

Facebook can be utilized as a springboard connecting authors to their public audience. Information specialists can embed links not only to market libraries but also to encourage their patrons as members or groups promoting their works. Since Facebook pages range from simple to detailed with unique photographs, archived events, and video features, librarians can assist writers who are establishing and building a social presence and develop the skills to evaluate this evolving platform.

College brainchild Mark Zuckerberg founded TheFacebook.com in 2004 while studying psychology at Harvard University (Philips 2007). Free of membership fees, Facebook spread beyond college campuses to anyone with an e-mail address. This Web site can be personalized with photos, videos, narrative posts, and creative flair. With more than a 10-year history, Facebook continues to support smartphone and other technological advancements. Librarians have learned to use Facebook and other social media to assist authors as they create, publish, and promote their work.

Public, private, and university libraries have created Facebook Web pages to reach clientele. Posts range from announcements to videos for recreational and educational purposes. Librarians can capture an audience via social media beyond the traditional nine-to-five business hours of operation. Images, text, and timelines enhance the abundance and flow of information.

The effect of America's 67 million baby boomers and their online habits is not nearly the influence of the 98 million people ages 7 to 29 in the millennial generation. These digital natives represent nearly one-third of the U.S. population (Chmielewski 2012). The implications of their networking patterns are colossal and challenging to predict accurately. Librarians may wish to stay abreast of this generation's interests because they are an elusive market for networks and advertisers to capture (Madrigal 2014).

College and university libraries incorporate Facebook to reach students, faculty, and affiliates to raise awareness about the collection and services. For instance, the Arizona State University Library (2015) offers publication services guiding writers through the selection of text, image, sound, video, and citation recommendations, transforming the media into a scholarly publication, exhibit, or Web page.

Academic libraries across the nation provide writing and publication direction. An example is the University of Washington Libraries Research Commons (2015). Librarians have created scholarly publishing guides to assist with research, writing, printing, and electronic publishing.

Colleges and universities typically offer graphic arts and copying options for traditional brochures, fliers, business cards, papers, and assorted printing services. In addition, college and university librarians can offer writing labs for tutoring students in their research projects, tailoring a message, or crafting a style while providing rhetorical strategies with accurate citations and composing convincing documents. The Purdue University (2015) Online Writing Lab (OWL) is a proven and reliable resource offering an academic writing foundation. Librarians can be an integral, innovative piece of the writing and publishing puzzle.

On the lighter side, the Lowrider Librarian Facebook page (Macias 2015) inspires readers with an interesting perspective about the culture and communication of libraries and learning. Librarians can serve as a partner in the evolution of social media posting, writing, and publishing.

Writers from the Kansas Authors Club utilized Facebook to collaborate on a book entitled *Green Bike*. Kevin Rabas, Mike Graves, and Tracy Million Simmons (2014) worked independently but posted their writing on a Facebook page open to local members of the Emporia Authors Group. In "About Green Bike," an appended section of the book, the authors wrote, "Later, we scraped the text from Facebook and formatted the novel ourselves using Adobe InDesign. However, scraping from Facebook sometimes introduced daunting formatting errors, which we took days or weeks cleaning up." They then self-published their work by orchestrating separately and in unison much like jazz improvisational solos.

MySpace

During the infancy of social media, MySpace gained the attention of young adults. "Teenagers have long been the vanguard of popular culture, which explains why so many adults are only now taking a close look at the social-network sites that young folks have been flocking to in recent years" (Scott 2006). MySpace (https://myspace.com) boasted more than 90 million accounts, primarily registered by teens. More recently this networking site attracts artists and musicians and supports on-demand listening and sharing. The Denver Public Library (2014) MySpace page offers connections to people, songs, radio stations, albums, videos, photos, articles, other libraries, and networking and musical opportunities.

Facebook, MySpace, and other social media platforms have the ability to transform an author's work into an ever-present conversation piece. Librarians can assist writers who wish to connect with friends, family, and potential customers on a variety of electronic stages (Gordon, Weir, and Girard 2014). Information about popular social networking Web pages can be accessed at Library Success: A Best Practices Wiki (2015). Writers collaborating with information specialists can attract their intended audience incorporating social media.

LinkedIn

Originally designed for the business world, LinkedIn is a social networking site for work-related conversations and job opportunities. Manage and enhance your professional network with this tool. Take advantage of tutorials making the most of your resources at ALA's LinkedIn Web page for librarians (American Library Association 2016b). Search for jobs, engage in dialogue, and reconnect with former colleagues. Cultivate collaboration, link globally, and establish relationships with others who share similar occupational, recreational, or educational goals.

By joining an electronic community, librarians and authors can reach a larger society, then branch into subcommunities of similar interests and work together; for example, you can connect your cookbook to chefs and dietitians. By constantly evaluating the social media marketplace, you can attract appropriate audiences.

RECORDED PRESENTATIONS

Librarians can assist authors in the publication and promotion of their writing by providing guidance in the creation, branding, editing, uploading, and publishing of their videos, connecting their audience and engaging potential readers. Linking libraries and writers with YouTube, TeacherTube, and similar video productions builds relationships and models current technology practices. Visual media creatively communicate to a broad spectrum of viewers and potential readers.

Videos

Capturing and preserving information in a motion picture format engages viewers and supplies a snapshot of the author's work. Computers, cameras, cell phones, and assorted electronic equipment offer the necessary tools to create videos intriguing readers and potential consumers. Forward-thinking librarians who value innovation can provide priceless interactions engaging authors who wish to enhance their works and attract a larger audience.

YouTube

Originated by Steve Chen in 2005, YouTube is a video-sharing Web site allowing an international community of users to search, watch, and upload videos (Scott 2015b). Acquired by Google in 2006, the YouTube Web site is a "broadcast yourself" service designed primarily for ordinary people who want to publish videos. Since people post YouTube videos worldwide, there is an extensive range of materials. Some examples include homemade movies, sports bloopers, unique experiences, and comical events caught on video. People also post instructional videos, such as step-by-step computer help, do-it-yourself guides, and other how-to procedures.

While YouTube can serve as a business platform, people typically visit the Web site for entertainment and information. Since people commonly carry digital cameras or cell phones with video recording capability, more events are now captured on video than ever before, creating an abundant collection of amusing and educational videos. Videos can be spontaneous or scripted like those posted by local book promotions or the Library of Congress (2016).

TeacherTube

In contrast to YouTube, TeacherTube and SchoolTube select and post appropriate content for certain ages and audiences. For books that have a school audience, consider Teacher-Tube. Content is safe and appropriate. Advertised as an educational learning community for teachers, students, and parents, TeacherTube is a subscription-based searchable warehouse of lessons, documents, audio resources, interactive videos, activities, classrooms, and groups for content that is curated. With a Pinterest-like dashboard (see the description of Pinterest below), TeacherTube offers groups connections, photos, and documents in chronological order for straightforward searches.

Librarians guide authors through the process of writing, editing, and publishing, and take advantage of the engaging collection of prompts and activities. Sample the featured videos and lessons at http://www.teachertube.com. By establishing a collaborative culture with writers, librarians can broadcast the educational benefits of these relationships with implications beyond the classroom.

SchoolTube

Endorsed by more than 20 national education associations, SchoolTube is an elementary through high school innovative video-sharing platform. Teachers and librarians can inspire budding authors by creating interviews with writers, illustrators, and artists. Students and adults can access numerous academic activities, lessons, and games. Only limited by the creator's imagination, the power of visual storytelling can captivate any audience. Teachers and librarians can encourage writers to witness and participate in this online presentation tool. If YouTube is blocked from a school's Internet connection or students are denied access, School

Tube provides a plethora of resources at http://www.schooltube.com. Writers marketing only through YouTube and Facebook should consider whether these sites are displayed in school and for students.

Book Trailers

Similar to movie previews, book trailers are videos created by publishers, authors, artists, readers, and librarians promoting books. These infomercials are typically less than a minute in length; however, there is no required time frame. Book trailers are digital book talks highlighting unique features of the plot, a suspenseful scene, or a comical event and advertise intriguing characters, settings, and situations. Authors will appreciate librarians who provide samples of book trailers and guide them through the design process. Discussion and training can be completed during individual or group tutorials, writing workshops, and publishing conferences. Popular and award-winning books are highlighted by Book Trailers for Readers (Harcleroe 2015).

Students can create book trailers as alternatives to written or oral book reports. When posted, authors can use these trailers to promote their books and increase distribution.

The Young Adult Library Services Association (YALSA) encourages teenagers to suggest their top 10 books at http://www.ala.org/yalsa/teenstopten. Libraries may offer promotional in-house or online contests or events allowing patrons to participate and recognize their favorite books similar to http://www.booktrailersforreaders.com/. Book trailers support a culture of reading, raise curiosity, and intrigue readers. Readers may also promote their favorite books through social media.

Vimeo

A video-sharing Web site, Vimeo (2016) may provide another media format for librarians and authors promoting and exchanging their work. Created in 2004 for personal and professional sharing, this community welcomes various topics and interests. Librarians can assist writers who wish to project a brand and identify strengths, talents, interests, and books. When launching a book promotion, Vimeo may be an animated or realistic tool geared toward a specific audience.

SHOWCASING STILL IMAGES

Programs that can be downloaded on a computer or smartphone are called apps. Although some are free and easily installed, some apps require purchase and special software. The American Library Association (2016a) highlights innovative applications for today's community of learners. The section below describes additional types of social media applications.

Dropbox

Collect, categorize, distribute, and store any type of text, photo, video, or music file for business or pleasure with Dropbox (https://www.dropbox.com). Create digital collages or slideshows featuring ordinary people completing amazing feats. Preserve historical events, save fond memories, and connect with your colleagues and family members.

Photos saved on Dropbox can be transformed into slideshows or embedded links on electronic newsletters, Web fliers, or Web sites. Users may work independently or collaborate with colleagues to share and update files with this free and versatile app. Although Dropbox is most commonly equated with multimedia features, the textbox tool provides options to design, compose, create, and exchange documents.

Piqora

Business professionals have joined Piqora (http://www.piqora.com) to locate, curate, and publish picture galleries. Not related to Dropbox, Piqora offers similar digital collages for promotional purposes writers may appreciate. Librarians and their clientele may utilize these features to market a potential audience.

Instagram

The inspiration for Instagram was merely to make phone photos appear clearer. Instagram was invented from a combination of its meaning, "instant" and "telegram" (Waters 2015a). The impetus was to efficiently upload photos as a means of improved communication according to Instagram's original slogan, "Capture and share the world's moments." This free social network does not require a computer; the service rests in the user's handheld device. Instagram can be employed to market recreational books or other topics having strong visual appeal. For example, food photography for a cookbook may attract a select audience.

Instagram is commonly found at various libraries including the Massachusetts Institute of Technology (https://instagram.com/mitpics) and the St. Louis Public Library (https://instagram.com/stlouispubliclibrary). Librarians can work with writers to utilize Instagram by incorporating the application in their Web sites and by helping authors organize their posts into appropriate categories to effectively reach select audiences.

Pinterest

Ben Silbermann, Evan Sharp, and Paul Sciarra created and founded the Pinterest Web site in 2009, and it was publicly available in 2010 for users to share and collect inspirational images. A "Pin it Forward" campaign in 2010 introduced users to Pinterest (Waters 2015b). The evolution of Pinterest continues, since participants and their needs change with time. The Pinterest community of approximately 60 million is intended to be friendly and spark creativity. Tutorials and library examples can be found at http://www.yalsa.ala.org/thehub/2012/11/12/pining-for-for-pinterest.

Much more than a digital scrapbook, Pinterest empowers people to express themselves through such interests as decorating, food, crafts, travel, and hobbies. As a free service, it lets users post favorite images or icons on an electronic bulletin board called a Pinboard (Miles and Lacey 2012). Limited only by imagination and time, members can use Pinterest to promote their brands and ideas. Sample locations for ideas include the Seattle Public Library (https://www.pinterest.com/seattlelibrary/) and the University of Nebraska–Lincoln (https://www.pinterest.com/unlincoln/).

Pinterest members can contact those interested in specific content, books, merchandise, or Web sites. Schedule Pin Alerts at http://www.pinalerts.com/index/login to receive e-mail messages. Pinreach (https://www.tailwindapp.com/pinreach) is now called Tailwind, a multiboard pinning board with shortcuts, analytics, and marketing for a subscription fee. Since Pinterest boards offer numerous functions and serve a variety of audiences, authors will appreciate librarians who inform, train, and suggest interesting and appropriate pins promoting their work on a complimentary or minimal cost basis.

Slideshare

Affiliated with LinkedIn, Slideshare (http://www.slideshare.net) is ideal for professionals who wish to integrate social media into library operations. By joining Slideshare, writers have the opportunity to experience valuable interactions, contribute to a support network, convey their tips and tribulations, and promote their work. Users can learn from shared conversations how to market and effectively communicate with their audience.

Flickr

A photojournalist, scrapbooker, writer, or camera whiz may appreciate Flickr (https://www.flickr.com), an online photo management and sharing system. A stream of photo albums can be explored free of advertisements. Similar to Pinterest, members save and share their photos and browse other photos and videos. Users also can create wall art and photo books from their images, capturing character and color promoting their works. Visit https://www.flickr.com/photos/cpsphotolibrary for examples.

Tumblr

David Karp, who believed that following blogs and sharing would improve the lives of others, invented Tumblr in 2007. When Karp devised tumblelogs, short blogging platforms, he thought weaving Web sites into the journals would enhance the sites and cater to bloggers and individuals who wrote comments. This advertisement-free Web site, known as an Internet forum, allows participants to view and communicate through threads or strings of messages (Jackson 2015).

The Tumblr screen is similar to an automobile dashboard with a simple format for ease of locating features. Private or personal information is not required in creating or maintaining an account. Users are permitted to submit multiple times daily or schedule when posts are visible.

The American Library Association Think Tank Tumblr account (http://alathinktank.tumblr.com) encourages pioneering and problem solving. Through anonymous conversations, followers view or participate in the question and answer scenarios. Writers and librarians can utilize Tumblr for its multimedia, microblogging platform, and social networking characteristics including music clips, animated images, stories, photos, art, and links. For authors who wish to attract readers and entice consumers, not only are interactive communication tools a substitution for traditional announcements, they augment contacts in today's interactive world.

INTERACTIVE COMMUNICATION TOOLS

If authors want to interact with their readers or other writers, social media can be used. By staying current with social media, a librarian can reach and assist clientele focusing on single or multiple forms of Web resources. These networks can be orchestrated to exude enthusiasm and a zest for learning and sharing. Some of the most supportive social media for writers comes from other writers. Interacting with authors, friends, and potential readers and fans provides a channel for complaints and compliments.

Digital analyst, anthropologist, author, and futurist Brian Solis (2016) is considered a leader in digital transformation; his conversation prism is a visual map of the social media landscape that graphically categorizes and represents applications for a variety of uses. This visual diagram categorizes and graphically presents the connectedness and application for use for authors or anyone considering utilizing social media. Authors and information professionals can study how people are talking and communicating to determine how to most effectively reach their intended audience.

Twitter

Jack Dorsey's inspiration to create Twitter was born from his fascination with trains, their network of tracks, and the "voice communication he heard over the police scanner as a child" (Scott 2015a). Twitter posts can be compared to precise dispatch language. Twitter, abbreviated as "twttr," was publicly available in 2006. A communication model, Twitter allows participants to broadcast or "tweet" messages; "tweets" are limited to 140 characters. Although an unregistered user can read the announcements, registered members can read and post or "retweet" messages.

Librarians who engage in social networking, blogging, or microblogging may recommend this communication tool to their writers who can attract followers with announcements and invitations. Expressing information in an efficient and practical manner makes this free tool user-friendly. A respected journal, *The Horn Book* (2015), remains current with traditional print and online book reviews, author and illustrator interviews, book awards, and publishing details. Follow @HornBook on Twitter for recent publication collections and tips.

Some librarians and authors contribute to literary discussion through social media. For instance, Joyce Kasma Valenza is noted for her Twitter account, blog, and Web site for all educators and librarians. Her TED Talks, research, outstanding programs, and presentations represent an energetic professional remaining current with interactive communication tools.

Twitter is an easy way to follow people and retweet what a person has written, resembling a fan club of earlier days. Now writers and their readers can share information electronically, creating a social media buzz online.

Listservs

Electronic mailing lists, commonly known as listservs, continue to grow in popularity. This Internet service brings together people with similar interests, occupations, contacts, or organizations. Monitored by an individual, select members, or the whole group, e-mail communication enables librarians and clientele to share information. For instance, the American Library Association hosts numerous electronic discussion lists that can be viewed at http://lists.ala.org/sympaalphabetically or by categories. Joining an email service of this nature typically is complimentary to all members of the organization.

Librarians, writers, illustrators, and other professionals may unite via listservs whether planning events and conferences, searching and posting job vacancies, creating and promoting books, or keeping current with technology trends. Listservs present a platform to exchange ideas, solve problems, and share best practices in ordinary or unique situations.

Blogs

Since a Weblog is a personal or team publishing Web site, a blogger is a digital author. In their book *Playing with Media*, authors Wes and Rachel Fryer (2011) state that we should play with digital text and digital media because we are digital natives and digital immigrants, and librarians represent this digital bridge. The Fryers' blog, *Moving at the Speed of Creativity* (http://www.speedofcreativity.org), captures the essence of effective communication. Librarians can empower their clientele to expand as multimedia conversationalists with this platform.

Follow *The Adventures of Library Girl* (blog) and learn from her voices from the trenches. Jennifer LaGarde weaves book discussions into real-life scenarios in addition to being a reading champion.

Sue Fitzgerald's *Unpretentious Librarian* blog (http://www.unpretentiouslibrarian.blogspot .com) is filled with reading, programming, and educational and promotional strategies ideal for most librarians and writers. Blogs have an enormous potential to captivate readers.

Blogs specifically geared toward educators, like EduBlog (edublog.org), are appropriate for a larger audience. *Building a Culture of Collaboration* (Collins, Green, Kaplan, and Moreillon 2015) is a blog promoting reading globally and locally. This blog includes current and archived contributions from writers, educators, and librarians.

The Global, History Educator blog (http://cperrier.edublogs.org) by Craig J. Perrier is complete with rich, academic resources, thought-provoking models, global intelligence competencies, and more. Information professionals can connect with authors refining and promoting their works in a blog framework. Any one of the aforementioned bloggers can also publish a book based on their posts.

A video log, known as a vlog, may include documentation of someone's life, works, and hobbies communicated for a specific audience. Author John Green's vlog (https://www .youtube.com/vlogbrothers) posts unique and interesting comments geared toward diverse readers including the Project for Awesome to raise awareness for various charities. Authors who wish to captivate bloggers may also connect with readers via vlogs.

Amanda Hovious (2015) created an instructional design and technology blog modeling knowledge of transmedia storytelling that may intrigue authors. Examples of mixing stories with digital elements can be viewed at https://designerlibrarian.wordpress.com. Authors interested in attracting a gaming audience may imitate this style as a springboard for their material.

The *Rocky Mountain Land Library* blog links the community to its resources and features physical and literal trails. Books, bees, and beautiful scenery cleverly contribute to this touching resource.

Buffy Hamilton has developed *The Unquiet Librarian* blog. This learning strategist, technology integration specialist, mover, and shaker posts inspirational items and presentations that can unite information specialists and writers.

Reviews and Marketing

A critical report or article in a journal evaluating a book or play is considered a review. Reviews evaluate and critique publications, providing compliments and criticisms of the manuscript. Librarians can assist clientele who wish to write reviews that identify the strengths and weaknesses of their written work. Clever and scholarly reviews attract the intended audience and engage potential readers. The American Library Association and most publishing companies post reviews in an effort to inform readers, allowing them to make informed purchasing decisions.

Typically libraries search for patrons and staff members to write reviews for a local newspaper and newsletter. By offering courses, supporting, and encouraging writing book reviews, patrons can feel they have contributed and are valued. These reviews can be posted on listservs, blogs, and social media, articulating and highlighting key components. Composing comments for book jacket covers can also be a marketing tool bringing writers and librarians together.

Blogger and WordPress opened the general public to writing and challenged traditional publishing. These companies invented a platform for people to compose and share their thoughts and words with assorted themes and templates. The connection between librarians and writers can comprise promotion of published works, composition of book reviews, and design of traditional print or digital presence. This collaborative effort adds dimension to creation and distribution. Today's information specialists have the opportunity to work with all patrons, completing assorted tasks utilizing various forms of technology like https://designerlibrarian.wordpress.com/. Authors who wish to attract a gaming audience may imitate this style as a springboard for their material.

The Rocky Mountain Land Library (https://landlibrary.wordpress.com) links the community to its resources through an online author forum that allows reader response.

Technorati

Since its launch, Technorati has transformed from a blog index and search engine to a publisher advertising platform serving Web sites optimizing digital advertising and publishing (http://technorati.com). This software platform helps publishers identify which advertisements are most beneficial and improves inventory control. Librarians can assist authors in a similar fashion by analyzing the intended audience and recommending appropriate marketing strategies. Technorati generates communication and inspires writers and librarians who wish to improve an image or enhance the written word.

BuzzFeed

Similar to a blog, BuzzFeed (http://www.buzzfeed.com/buzz) is a social news and entertainment Internet media company that offers "content-driven publishing technology" for pleasure browsing. Members can view and post videos, quizzes, and news. This community encourages all writers to contribute.

BuzzFeed is a popular location including curious topics, current quizzes, and silly videos. Information specialists and authors who are interested in engaging this playful audience may benefit from "buzzing in" the conversation.

Reddit

A social news Web site, Reddit (https://www.reddit.com) accepts stories curated and promoted by site members. Join this site to view subcommunities, known as "subreddits." With numerous categories such as gadgets, music, and philosophy, Reddit site members, also known as "redditors," submit content that is voted on by other members. Writing prompts motivate participation. The purpose is to send the most pertinent stories to the top of the site's main thread page. Libraries may consider incorporating this conversational Web site to attract the millennial generation.

Webinars

Like many of these interactive communication tools, conference calls provide a method of bringing like minds together; webinars serve a similar purpose. A webinar, or Web-based seminar, may be a lecture or workshop transmitted over the Internet with interactive features allowing participants to give and receive information. Visual details may be presented online in addition to real-time conversation orally or in a chat box.

Authors wishing to attract a larger audience may utilize webinars promoting their books, publications, speaking events, or service projects. In addition to hosting onsite events raising awareness about author engagements, book signings, and programs, libraries can offer webinars for their patrons. Bestselling author James Patterson teamed with professional basketball player Dwayne Wade and other NBA stars sharing how reading has shaped their lives. These free webinars have been hosted in public shopping malls and other locations, and archived sessions are available at http://www.readkiddoread.com.

Like other writers, James Patterson offers reading incentives and writing workshops. Libraries can orchestrate similar inspirational sessions for small or large groups. Since librarians tend to respect and admire writers, they are unique at building relationships. When a personal visit is not feasible, polished or novice authors will appreciate the opportunity to showcase their work and connect with others in webinar settings. Participants can view webinars alone or in groups in private or public settings, making them more available. Librarians can broadcast existing webinars or feature local successful writers in their own webinars.

Although some software installation may be required in creating, hosting, and attending webinars, free or low-cost packages are available for local and international meetings. For example, WebJunction (2016) is a source for informative tutorials covering numerous library-related topics. Librarians can facilitate these gatherings bringing people of similar interests together in an effort to be more than a book butler and demonstrate professional development.

Podcasts

Recorded presentations serve multiple functions in a world of evolving online discussions and exchanges. Often podcasts are audio only, but some are both audio and video. Similar to a webinar, a podcast is typically a video file or audio recording that can be downloaded from a Web site. A podcast is usually geared toward selected participants with a specific theme. Innovative information specialists and writers can create live podcasts. Searchable and accessible archived audio and video interviews and programs promote reading. For instance, middle grades author Angela Cervantes was interviewed by a librarian to produce a podcast posted on their library Web page (Ericsson 2015).

Richard Saul Wurman originated the TED Conference, a "powerful convergence among three fields: technology, entertainment, and design that included a demo of the compact disc, the e-book, and cutting-edge 3D graph" (TED Talks 2014). The TED Conference evolved into numerous TED programs and initiatives fostering open-mindedness and curiosity; TED Talks share discovery and spawn conversation.

COLLABORATIVE COMMUNITIES

In their book *The Art of Social Media: Power Tips for Power Users*, Kawasaki and Fitzpatrick (2014) recognize the value of consolidating media forms—blogs, Facebook, Twitter, YouTube, and RSS feeds into one virtual workspace like Socialtext (http://www.socialtext.com). A subscription-based communication sharing pictures, images, documents, and various attachments can enhance workflow and improve collaboration.

Another example of consolidating media is Huddle (https://www.huddle.com), which allows subscribers to create secure workspace in streamlined cloud collaboration to share content. Visit Huddle for customization of research, reports, blogs, infographics, videos, webinars, and white papers.

Tony Wagner (2012) recommends reimagining occupations, since technology transforms learning and jobs. Innovation is essential for lifelong learning, and librarians can be leaders teaming with other professionals. His research can positively impact writers and readers.

Mastering time, juggling media, and avoiding distractions, librarians and authors can follow Peter Bregman's (2011) approach to navigate the continual chatter of digital correspondence to improve production. Information specialists and writers can benefit from these organizational tips for staying focused on the truly important tasks.

Social media allows writers and librarians to design their own content and virtually share with others. Toolkits, brochures, and reliable resources raise awareness, assisting professionals and patrons in making informed digital decisions. Librarians can leave a lasting legacy with their guidance and support.

BEST PRACTICES

Today's libraries have the opportunity to distinguish themselves from the traditional book warehouse. Librarians can offer programs, events, and resources arming writers with skills to create, publish, and promote their works.

Numerous organizations recognize libraries and authors for their efforts to foster creativity in their communities. Each year the American Library Association (ALA) honors books and videos. Recognized for their quality, the ALA Youth Media Awards include the Newbery, Caldecott, Printz, and Coretta Scott King Book Awards. Details are available at www.ala.org/yma. These awards encourage creative work in children's and young adult literature and media (American Library Association 2016a). Writers and illustrators are recognized for their unique, touching, impressive publications.

The American Library Association also identifies dozens of accolades for accomplished libraries for their innovative events, training programs, branding, technology integration, and community connections. Recognizing resourceful and novel approaches to academic research and problem solving is the impetus behind the Innovation in Science and Technology Librarianship Award. The American Library Association recognized the Distributed Data Curation Center (D2C2) Research Department of the Purdue University Libraries for their research allowing librarians to access and utilize specific data.

For its "Meme Your Library" campaign, the Craighead County Jonesboro (Arkansas) Public Library earned the John Cotton Dana Library Public Relations Award for effective strategic communication. Due to inspirational technology and marketing strategies, the popular and humorous billboards, advertisements, postcards, and e-cards resulted in increased usage both physically and virtually. Learn more at http://www.ala.org/awardsgrants.

Recognizing partnerships between school librarians and teachers is the criterion for the Collaborative School Library Award that honors educators who have worked together utilizing library resources. The American Association of School Librarians (AASL) awarded school librarians Stephanie Meurer and Jennifer Milstead and language arts teacher Erin Kelley from Sierra Middle School in Parker, Colorado, for their joint curricular project of curated pictures, fiction, poetry, and video exhibits. Their efforts extended student learning beyond the classroom.

The National School Library Program of the Year Award recognizes school library programs ensuring students and staff are effective users of information and implementing AASL's learning standards. "Exemplary school library programs empower learners to be critical thinkers, enthusiastic readers, skillful researchers, and ethical users of information" (AASL 2015). Guidelines are available at http://www.ala.org/aasl/awards. Blue Valley High School (Stilwell, Kansas) was the AASL 2015 recipient for their service-oriented opportunities improving student achievement. Librarians Ken Stewart and Jessica Edwards have designed college and career readiness projects and LibGuides exemplifying their commitment to building partnerships. Their efforts composing and disseminating information demonstrate a willingness to assist others in various writing and publishing ventures.

An innovative learning space, YOUmedia, at 11 Chicago Public Library locations emphasizes digital media and the maker movement. Teens engage in a variety of media projects including graphic design, photography, video, and music. YOUmedia connects young adults with mentors and institutions throughout Chicago to encourage collaboration and creativity (Chicago Public Library 2016).

"Investing in Experiences" is the slogan of Seattle Public Library (http://www.spl.org). Although public libraries commonly offer digital citizenship and basic computer classes, the Seattle Public Library provides social media workshops including LinkedIn and Twitter. Topics include making connections, managing LinkedIn and Twitter accounts, creating a profile, mining contacts to identify hiring managers, finding jobs, and maximizing the network to develop key relationships. Not only is the architectural structure unique, the community connections are exceptional.

Comparable to academic institutes globally, the University of Washington Libraries (http://www.lib.washington.edu) provides connections including a Research Writing Commons where students physically and electronically collaborate with librarians on their projects. Learning labs assist patrons discovering and applying information.

A Learning Studio at a University of Kansas library is a dynamic research hub for undergraduate and graduate students and professors. Librarians, technology experts, and academics support students exploring and researching (https://lib.ku.edu/learningstudio).

CHAPTER SUMMARY

Social media have entered the mainstream and can be used to foster collaboration in writing, publishing, and promoting self-published books and other publications. Librarians can create and support a culture of reading and writing through creative use of new technologies and social media. Social networking resources like Facebook and LinkedIn can be utilized to build collaborative writing communities. The Internet and newer technologies are readily available to enable professional presentations employing audio and video recordings to promote publications. Interactive communication tools, including listservs and blogs, expand the potential for writers to promote interactive communication with their audience.

Librarians can collaborate with authors to utilize these and emerging resources as they become available to enhance all aspects of self-publishing.

REFERENCES

American Association of School Librarians. 2015. http://www.ala.org/aasl/awards. Accessed November 7, 2015.

American Library Association. 2016a. Awards, Grants and Scholarships. http://www.ala.org/awardsgrants.

American Library Association. 2016b. LinkedIn for Librarians. http://www.ala.org/onlinelearning/linkedIn-librarians.

Arizona State University. ASU Libraries Publication and Creative Services. 2015. http://www.asu.edu/lib/archives/creative.htm. Accessed December 1, 2015.

Book Trailers for Readers. 2016. http://www.booktrailersforreaders.com/home.

Bregman, Peter. 2011. *18 Minutes: Find Your Focus, Master Distraction, and Get the Right Things Done*. New York: Hatchette Book Group.

Chicago Public Library. 2016. YOUmedia. http://www.chipublib.org/youmedia.

Chmielewski, D. C. 2012. "Digital Disruption: Changing Channels." *Los Angeles Times*, June 17. Retrieved from http://sks.sirs.com. Accessed July 19, 2015.

Collins, Karla, Lucy Santos Green, Judy Kaplan, and Judi Moreillon. 2015. Building a Culture of Collaboration to Support Student and Educator Success. http://buildingacultureofcollaboration.edublogs.org. Accessed December 11, 2015.

Denver Public Library MySpace. 2014. https://myspace.com/denver_evolver. Accessed October 16, 2015.

Ericsson, Miranda. 2015. "Hush Library Podcast #81—Angela Cervantes." October 11. http://tscpl.org/books-movies-music/hush-library-podcast-81-angela-cervantes.

Fitzgerald, Sue. 2015. *Unpretentious Librarian* (blog). http://www.unpretentiouslibrarian.blogspot.com. Accessed October 17, 2015.

Fryer, Wesley A. *Moving at the Speed of Creativity* (blog). http://www.speedofcreativity.org. Accessed October 17, 2015.

Fryer, Wesley A., and Rachel C. Fryer. 2011. *Playing with Media: Simple Ideas for Powerful Sharing*. Speed of Creativity Learning.

Gordon, Cindy, Andrew Weir, and John P. Girard. 2014. *Social Roots: Why Social Innovations Are Creating the Influence Economy*. New York: Business Expert Press.

Habley, Jennifer. 2015. "Stephanie Meurer, Jennifer Milstead and Erin Kelley Receive AASL Collaborative School Library Award for Holocaust Project." http://www.ala.org/news/press-releases/2015/05/stephanie-meurer-jennifer-milstead-and-erin-kelley-receive-aasl-collaborative. Accessed November 7, 2015.

Hamilton, Buffy. 2015. *The Unquiet Librarian* (blog). https://theunquietlibrarian.wordpress.com. Accessed December 13, 2015.

Harcleroe, Michelle. 2015. Book Trailers for Readers. http://www.booktrailersforreaders.com/Profile+on++Michelle+Harclerode. Accessed October 17.

The Horn Book. 2015. https://www.hbook.com. Accessed November 3, 2015.

Hovious, Amanda. 2015. *Designer Librarian: A Blog about Instructional Design and Technology in Libraries*. https://designerlibrarian.wordpress.com. Accessed November 3, 2015.

Jackson, Aurelia. 2015. *Tumblr: How David Karp Changed the Way We Blog*. Broomall, PA: Mason Crest.

Kawasaki, Guy, and Peg Fitzpatrick. 2014. *The Art of Social Media: Power Tips for Power Users*. New York: Portfolio/Penguin.

LaGarde, Jennifer. 2015. *The Adventures of Library Girl* (blog). http://www.librarygirl.net. Accessed July 18, 2015.

Library of Congress. 2016. YouTube. https://www.youtube.com/user/LibraryOfCongress.

Library Success: A Best Practices Wiki. 2015. Social Networking Software. http://www.libsuccess.org/Social_Networking_Software. Accessed November 7, 2015.

Macias, Max. 2015. *Lowrider Librarian*. Facebook. https://www.facebook.com/LowriderLibrarian. Accessed December 3, 2015.

Madrigal, A. 2014. "The Fall of Facebook." *Atlantic Monthly*, 34+. Retrieved from http://sks.sirs.com. Accessed June 19, 2015.

Miles, Jason G., and Karen Lacey. 2012. *Pinterest Power: Market Your Business, Sell Your Product, and Build Your Brand on the World's Hottest Social Network*. New York: McGraw-Hill.

MySpace.com. 2011. "MySpace Unleashes World's Largest Online Music Library to Fans Everywhere with New Music Player." December 20. http://www.prnewswire.com. Accessed October 16, 2015.

Patterson, James. 2015. http://readkiddoread.com. Accessed October 16, 2015.

Perrier, Craig J. 2015. *The Global, History Educator* (blog). http://cperrier.edublogs.org. Accessed December 11, 2015.

Philips, Sarah. 2007. "A Brief History of Facebook." *Guardian*, July 25. http://www.theguardian.com/technology/2007/jul/25/media.newmedia. Accessed July 18, 2015.

Piqora. 2015. http://www.piqora.com. Accessed September 20, 2015.

Purdue University. 2015. The Purdue Online Writing Lab. https://owl.english.purdue.edu. Accessed December 1.

Rabas, Kevin, Mike Graves, and Tracy Million Simmons. 2014. *Green Bike*. San Bernardino, CA: Meadowlark.

Reddit.com. 2015. https://www.reddit.com. Accessed October 15, 2015.

Rocky Mountain Land Library: A Resource Linking Land and Community (blog). 2015. https://landlibrary.wordpress.com. Accessed December 11.

SchoolTube. 2013. http://www.schooltube.com. Accessed October 17, 2015.

Scott, Celicia. 2015a. *Twitter: How Jack Dorsey Changed the Way We Communicate*. Broomall, PA: Mason Crest.

Scott, Celicia. 2015b. *YouTube: How Steve Chen Changed the Way We Watch Videos*. Broomall, PA: Mason Crest.

Scott, S. 2006. "Safeguard Your Reputation While Socially Networking." *PC World*, October 1 (10), 152. Retrieved from http://elibrary.bigchalk.com. Accessed September 20, 2015.

Solis, Brian. 2016. The Conversation Prism (Brian Solis + Jess3). https://conversationprism.com.

TeacherTube. 2015. http://www.teachertube.com. Accessed June 20, 2015.

TED Talks. 2014. History of TED. https://www.ted.com/about/our-organization/history-of-ted. Accessed October 17, 2015.

Thomsett-Scott, Beth C., ed. 2014. *Marketing with Social Media: A LITA Guide*. Chicago, IL: American Library Association.

University of Washington. University Libraries. Research Commons. 2015. http://www.lib.washington.edu/commons. Accessed December 1.

Valenza, Joyce Kasman. 2015. https://twitter.com/joycevalenza. Accessed November 1, 2015.

Vimeo. 2016. https://vimeo.com.

Wagner, Tony. 2012. *Creating Innovators: The Making of Young People Who Will Change the World*. New York: Scribner. http://www.tonywagner.com/resources/creating-innovators. Accessed June 20, 2015.

Waters, Rosa. 2015a. *Instagram: How Kevin Systrom and Mike Krieger Changed the Way We Take and Share Photos*. Broomall, PA: Mason Crest.

Waters, Rosa. 2015b. *Pinterest: How Ben Silbermann and Evan Sharp Changed the Way We Share What We Love*. Broomall, PA: Mason Crest.

WebJunction. 2016. https://www.webjunction.org.

OPEN ACCESS AND LIBRARIES

CHAPTER OVERVIEW

The Internet is spurring a Web publishing revolution. Information is becoming more openly available and accessible in a convenient online environment, stimulating a growing demand for timely access to information. This demand also involves information or research that is scholarly in nature.

What is Open Access? The Association of Research Libraries (2012) defines Open Access "as the dissemination of scientific and scholarly research literature online, free of charge, and free of unnecessary licensing restrictions." Academic libraries are working with the academy to provide publishing solutions. Who makes up the academy? The academy is the higher education community that includes a college or university institution, the researchers, faculty, academic professionals, administrators, staff, and students.

Open Access brings a new paradigm to the academy—a new value system and approach to publishing. The mission of higher education has long been to create new knowledge and disseminate it widely—through the acts of conducting research and teaching. The growth in digital software, tools, and the Open Access movement is drawing libraries and information professionals into providing solutions to disruptions in the scholarly communication system.

This chapter provides an overview of the Open Access movement and will address developing publishing services related to building digital collections, technological infrastructure, new personnel, and practices. Desktop publishing software has grown to spur new models of publishing. The Open Access movement has encouraged rethinking and restructuring of the research, dissemination, and publishing processes.

As the access to information and new knowledge is made more widely available, the opportunity for learning is further democratized, cutting across economic, social, political, and cultural lines. As the access to information becomes more readily available, so does the opportunity to be an author. An evolution is underway in which the opportunity to discover, learn, discuss, create, and disseminate digital work is stimulating an evolution in publishing—an evolution made possible by an Open Access movement. Academic libraries provide leadership in this movement, leveraging partnerships and opportunities for collaboration with other types of libraries and their communities.

OVERVIEW OF THE OPEN ACCESS MOVEMENT

The Culture of Scholarly Publishing

Faculty members in the academy pursue a research agenda that is designed to add new knowledge to our society through the rigor of scholarly inquiry. Faculty members pursue publication of their research and/or creative works and have traditionally published as they pursue tenure and promotion. The rigor of this culture also serves to evaluate the impact of faculty members through their research endeavors and within the lens of their discipline.

The requirement to contribute to the scholarly record is a process that has its challenges. Many have referred to the phrase "publish or perish" as it relates to the expectations of the academy and the life of college and university professors. Faculty are engaged in teaching courses, pursuing research funds (often as federally funded grants), conducting research publishing those findings, and providing service (to the institution, the academic disciplines, and to allied associations). The culture of research publishing is directly related to the academic mission in today's colleges and research institutions.

Scholarly publishing differs in comparison to popular publishing or the publishing market that supports a genre that will generate the highest profit and reach the largest public demand. Once research has been published in a research journal, it might later become part of a book written for the general public. A glance at the *New York Times* Nonfiction Best Sellers List, for example, shows titles on recent research in science, health, and economics. In other words, books on topics such as climate change, brain health, and sustainability have made the list. These books report research findings, what those findings mean for our wider society, and recommendations for changing our behavior in order to benefit from the understanding that comes as a result of those research investigations from the academy. In addition to books, popular media such as newscasts also report the research findings published in top-tier research journals. This trend can be seen during the nightly news when health information is reported in the mainstream media.

Scholarly Communications

The scholarly communication system is the wider process by which ideas are crafted into a work, reviewed and edited, published and reproduced in number, made available for purchase, and disseminated to others who then read, learn, and reformulate those ideas into new publications. When an item is produced or published, it undergoes a process of review. Scholarly works by their very nature are peer-reviewed, then edited, and published. The traditional publishing model is a linear process that involves relationships among libraries, authors, and publishers. It has been a long-standing interwoven symbiotic culture that has served traditional scholarly publishing well until now.

Disruptions and the Dawning of the Open Access Movement

Several disruptions of the traditional scholarly communication system have contributed to the Open Access movement. The increased enrollment at the end of World War

II in many colleges and universities challenged the academy to answer the increased need of GIs headed to college, leveraging their GI Bill and increasing the number of educated citizens. As the academy grew, so did our global communication and technological infrastructure. Meanwhile, our cultural demand for rapid delivery of financial and medical information also grew. When the World Wide Web opened for business and public use in the early 1990s, the demand for rapid delivery of communication and data documents continued to grow, driving use of the Internet. In addition, the cost of scholarly publications also began to rise and has continued to grow, outpacing academic library budgets.

The Open Access movement has grown from a focus on the philosophical value of sharing information to a movement beyond advocacy and to one of action where valuable research findings are made widely available to the general public. The Open Access movement now embraces practical applications supported by real-time need, a reality due to the increasing costs of academic research journals, shrinking library budgets, diminishing price competition and consolidation of publishers, and the expectation that access to research findings is needed in a timely manner (Crawford 2011). Currency is critical for science information, and print does not stay current with trends.

Reasons the Open Access Movement Has Grown

- The Internet has provided a means for disseminating information.
- The cost of academic research journals has risen.
- The public and private sectors have increased expectations for timely access to publicly funded research findings.
- Academic library budgets are shrinking.
- Publishing companies have consolidated, resulting in diminished price competition.
- Research findings double every 66 days.
- Current information from medical research doubles every 33 days.
- Authors interested in teaching and learning are willing to share their work widely.
- Multiple researchers engage in collaborative projects that demand data management and sharing over long geographical distances.
- The culture of some scientific disciplines requires the sharing of findings while research is in progress; this sharing further informs current research projects and innovation.

Most of the strides in Open Access publishing have been made with journals. Numerous studies have shown Open Access publishing increases citation impact. For additional information about implementing Open Access, see the Open Access Scholarly Information Sourcebook (OASIS 2015). There are two commonly used models of scholarly Open Access publishing that have emerged—Gold and Green. The Gold model, also known as the Author Pays model, involves publishers who pass on the cost of Open Access publishing to the author directly, requiring an Author Publishing Charge or APC. APCs run an estimated $1,000 to $5,000 fee that is paid in advance of the publishing.

Green publishing allows authors to retain their author rights to archive their publications in their institutional repository or another Open Access repository. For example, the Social Science Research Network encourages early release of research results and is a multidisciplinary online repository that collects working papers. In the literature a Platinum model has also been used to refer to the ideal or fully open publication that offers works openly and freely.

Open Access requires a technological infrastructure that is not free, but the idea persists that Platinum publishing does not charge an author fee and that the costs are handled as subsidies through grants, benevolence, or the volunteer work of others. Over the years some scholars have been doubtful that such an ideal can be achieved. Today this model is in use by some in the science, math, and health fields, but it still is not the norm.

The Platinum model is the ideal to move toward, but it takes time to create such large-scale publishing ventures. However, we are beginning to see movement in this area. For example, the *Open Journal of Astrophysics* (2016) is a Platinum publishing model that holds no APC or subscription fees. All of the articles hold a Creative Commons Attribution license, making them free to authors and readers. The accepted peer-reviewed articles receive a Digital Object Identifier and citations are accessed through CrossRef (2015) like other journals.

Some are quick to mention that faculty members are the producers and the consumers of the scholarly work. Faculty members are the authors, editors, and peer-reviewers of scholarly publications. As authors they also consume or use published materials that academic libraries purchase and make available for consumption and use. Academic scholars rely on and engage with publications and research findings in order to reformulate and create new scholarly articles, books, and other works. Faculty also provide service in their disciplines as editors and peer reviewers serving on editorial boards for journals and reviewing books in their specialized research areas. Faculty provide a key role in producing valued publications that are then purchased by the libraries in academic institutions.

Motivations and Benefits of Open Access Publishing

The act of disseminating scholarly works as widely as possible involves more than a philosophical desire to democratize access. It involves a cultural and technological infrastructure that supports the tenure and promotion cycle. Royalties do not drive scholarly publishing; however, this isn't to say that financial gain for faculty authors doesn't matter. Scholarly publishing is based on the values of prestige, scientific discovery, creation of new knowledge, and the contribution or impact to the benefit of the academy and the wider society.

Open Access advocates acknowledge that the traditional scholarly communication system is failing the academy—the very scholars whose publications, editorial, and review efforts comprise the heart of the system. The current civil discourse addresses the reality that it is the publishers who make a large financial gain on the hard work of today's faculty. It is hard to see a monetary gain for faculty when academic salaries have not kept up with inflation. Meanwhile, scholarly publishing costs have skyrocketed beyond academic library budgets, making it impossible for libraries to provide access to some of the top-tier journals that researchers need in order to conduct research.

The culture of research encourages scholars to build upon earlier work, to reformulate and create new knowledge that can be vetted and trusted as quality work. The traditional scholarly communication model in which universities support academic authors,

> ### The Benefits of Open Access Publishing to Scholars, Researchers, Authors, and Publishers
>
> - Equal access to scholarly research for those at wealthy and poor institutions
> - Rapid dissemination of scholarly research findings
> - Increased availability of research in progress and other gray literature
> - Recognition of others engaged in similar investigations
> - Strengthened ongoing research by forming intentional communities that support information sharing and cross-disciplinary research collaborations
> - Increased readership beyond discipline-based peer group
> - Increased citation by both those in the academy and in the private sector
> - Improved ethical integrity of science due to open data sets and new opportunities for others to do data analysis, replication, and additional research
> - Cost savings benefits:
>   - Lessening the APC charge
>   - Providing cheaper access through the Internet
>   - Decreasing the cost of a college education with open textbooks

publishing companies publish academic research, and libraries buy back the publications as costs increase, has evolved into a barrier for the academic and scholarly communication process. This barrier no longer makes sense, especially during a time when the Web provides a radically simplified location that supports worldwide dissemination. It is now possible to track article views and citations with Google Analytics and Google Scholar, making scholarly research more available and accessible to the individual. The Web is a natural tool to foster data integrity within the academic research culture.

A Convergence in the Open Movement

Change is inevitable. The Open Access movement is gaining momentum. New publishing models are emerging. Among these models are academic libraries that are building digital scholarship services where librarians work to provide solutions for scholars during the changing publishing landscape. A new type of librarian will be addressed later in the chapter. The ongoing evolution in the open movement has led to Open Access, Open Education, Open Government, Open Data, and Open Educational Resources (OERs).

Open Access involves the scientific community, higher education, researchers, and the public as U.S. policies mandate that federally funded research must be made openly available to the public. The technological advances with the infrastructure of the Web and open software platforms in recent years have made discovery and distribution of research or new knowledge more accessible than ever. Federal funding agencies now require researchers to make their findings accessible in Open Access journals, which have grown significantly in number.

Universities are adopting policies mandating that their researchers post a copy of their published work in repositories accessible to the public. This practice changes the way scholarly content is made available and supports the wider philosophical mission of colleges and universities whose scholars desire broad dissemination of their scholarly work. Authors now gain greater dissemination of research findings, thus furthering the advancement of new knowledge.

Providing public access to federally funded research is a legal mandate that originated from legislation including the National Institutes of Health (NIH) Public Access Policy of 2008 and the more recent 2010 Federal Research Public Access Act. The potential users of such research have a variety of benefits from these policies that are making progress establishing an open culture where all potential users have free and timely access to peer-reviewed federal research findings on the Internet. The NIH public access policy benefits America's citizens by providing timely access to relevant scientific information, informing clinical care, stimulating discovery, and improving health literacy. The Modern Language Association and Association of Academic Health Sciences Libraries have observed firsthand the significant benefit of providing public access to publications arising from NIH-funded research including its positive cost-benefit ratio, return on investment, and efficacy and efficiency to fuel new research, discoveries, and therapies.

Benefits extend outside the medical community to other disciplines, extending into commerce and to the general public where research findings influence society in the broadest sense. As access to published research becomes democratized and available to every sector in society, the research benefits also grow. For example, when a state university's agriculture program distributes the findings of their research, local farmers and ranchers can adjust their practices for higher yields and healthier livestock.

The Benefits of Open Access Publishing to Society

- Equal access to information for all Internet users
- Transparency in the spending of federal research dollars
- Application of research findings to increase learning for K–12 students
- STEAM learning activities spurred by OER curricula
- Lifesaving medical information openly available to the public through PubMed Central and other repositories
- Application of cross-disciplinary research to problems related to mental health, the human condition, city planning and infrastructure, food and water supplies, and other issues facing cities in the twenty-first century
- Access to research by scientists in the private sector in order to stimulate innovation
- Access to research by entrepreneurs to develop products and services that further enhance a community's economic growth

---

The open movement has had significant growth. Librarians have come to recognize the principles of intellectual freedom and librarianship through the expansive perspective of information policy. American democracy and our wider global information community have provided increased access to knowledge, and some see the open movement as a great equalizer, providing opportunity and stimulating innovation.

During the fall of 2011, the Berlin 9 International Conference on Open Access was held in Washington, D.C. It was the first of its kind in the United States and was co-hosted by the

Scholarly Publishing and Academic Resources Coalition (SPARC), an international alliance of academic and research libraries working to create a more open system of scholarly communication (SPARC 2015).

Since then, the North American Open Access Conference has been held multiple times every other spring. It brings together policymakers, librarians, researchers, students, leaders in the publishing industry, and academic administrators with compelling case studies. SPARC recognizes that the open movement is converging in many areas, including Open Access, Open Data, and the creation, dissemination, and use of OERs.

The open movement has reached a tipping point. Librarians within the academy will continue to serve as the bridge from traditional publishing practices to support for open solutions. The growth of a wider scholarly communication system will offer deeper connections to scholarly works and provide a digital identity of the whole researcher. Such a digital footprint could reveal the influence of their mentors, other scholars, and the related work of those outside their discipline.

DEVELOPING PUBLISHING SERVICES

The Open Access movement is increasing the impact of research through policies, practices, and the onset of new technological tools, creating additional opportunities to advance research and creative endeavors. Some academic libraries are embracing a renewed idea of the library as publisher. For more information on the traditional publishing system, refer to Chapters 3 and 4 of this book.

The growing role of scholarly publishing among academic librarians is one of creation that engages scholars in both their research and creative endeavors, as well as in their work in scholarly publishing. This innovation is taking place in the digital sphere. Higher education institutions historically without a university press are creating a digital press and offering a variety of services focused on open dissemination.

New services require changes in the organizational structure. Reorganization in several institutions looks something like highly fluid teams whose work is positioned to welcome and meet the educational needs of users and to build upon relationships with subject faculty colleagues with regard to their research and grant work to engage as research partners. The increasing focus is on supporting research investigations in the academy and making the wider scholarly communication system an important priority for libraries. This change involves shifting resources, talent, and our definitions of success. Success can be recognized through a culture of learning that spans across functioning work teams positioned around an initiative instead of around traditional departmental work. This structure supports leaders throughout the organization and further disrupts long-time silos in favor of more fluid workflows that support consultation and digital project management.

Collection Building and the Infrastructure for a Digital Repository

The library as publisher includes the creation of local research collections and the work to disseminate those collections widely through a digital repository, a storage place. Digital repositories can be archives, a place for digital items when the copyright, permissions, or license is not available for public use. This is known as a "dark archive." Or a digital repository can be an Open Access repository where the content is available for wide dissemination through the Web. Open repositories increase the visibility and discoverability of scholarly and creative works, encourage collaboration and innovation, and contribute to the ongoing development of new knowledge.

Many academic institutions are investing their financial and personnel resources in an institutional repository (IR). IR is an earlier term for what academic librarians have come to recognize as a group of digital repositories and services. In large research universities an IR may be made of several digital repositories, one for scholarly articles, one for data, and another for cultural heritage items. This separation is due to the variety of digital files and early limitations of the repository software and servers used to store and make the works available. Such technological infrastructure needs a level of compatibility in order to provide secure backups for storage, wide discoverability online, and the increased use that leads to reuse.

Commercial vendors, who serve as a third party, provide a hosted solution. Such repository software and service innovations make an IR possible for smaller institutions with limited resources. Larger research libraries are naturally positioned to build robust IR infrastructures that can address the growing need that comes from managing an Open Access repository. Content might include a variety of scholarship from gray matter, published articles, data sets, and other dynamic digital research, databases, and scholarly outputs.

Skilled personnel are required to build a repository. For example, there are programming, work, and copyright considerations to be made when building an Open Access repository. Some choices include leveraging a variety of open source software and tools that require programming. Copyright consultation and policy creation is a dynamic and involved area of library publishing services. Regardless of size, institutions will want to consider current copyright practices and author rights issues when investigating their options for building digital library publishing services. When an IR is solely under the control of a state-funded institution, the Fair Use Exemption to the U.S. Copyright Law can apply. Having technical trained personnel gives the institution the ability to provide needed flexibility and customization required in building a robust IR.

Necessary tools and digital innovations can be realized through research partnerships and may include new digital research methodologies used by scholars in the digital humanities. Libraries, collaborative by nature, are focused on programming solutions that provide customized uses of a variety of open source software and related plug-ins in order to work in partnership on research endeavors across the academy. Successful projects have been realized by those recipients of National Endowment for the Humanities research grants. For example, the Walt Whitman Archive is an online resource that provides convenient access to information about Whitman's life and includes a variety of works, a gallery of images, letters, and related articles (Price and Folsom 2015). The archive involves professors and students, technical consultants, contributing editors, and advisory board members on this large multi-institution project.

New Type of Librarian

In the academy new roles for librarians are emerging. In the changing scholarly communication system new positions are focused on research, publishing, and such related items as data. Providing services in the changing landscape of scholarly publishing places libraries in the innovative role of the library as publisher.

The librarians whose work focuses on scholarly communications are a new breed of librarian that connects library departments with new policies and practices that require breaking down the traditionally separate departments and working across departmental lines. These librarians lead from the middle and manage projects that span many departments in the library to accomplish their work. Some institutions have recognized that this work involves a more unified approach in which a scholarly communications unit has been organized to include instruction liaisons with strong faculty relationships and a public service focus, digital project librarians with strong technological skill sets (such as open source software, digital repository, metadata, and information management skills), copyright and intellectual property rights expertise for education and policy creation, and a focus on providing publishing services for the academy.

New software that moves beyond the desktop publishing of yesterday to include open publishing software tools is adding to an emerging narrative of the library as publisher. New publishing models are emerging, and digital repository software use and publishing services are growing across the academy. Librarians are broadening their set of skills by learning project management, social media usage, Geographic Information System (GIS) and data visualization, search engine optimization, data analytics, copyright, author rights and intellectual property rights, digital research methodologies, research data management software and practices, policy creation, and the art of designing Open Access journals. Library publishing involves traditional text, as well as multimedia and the creation of 3D images.

This work began in offices and conference rooms and has grown as libraries are expanding into prime real estate areas of the library. A growing trend is to construct new digital scholarship centers with collaborative learning and creation spaces. Recent case studies demonstrate the work underway at Brown University and McMaster University (Lippincott, Hemmasi, and Lewis 2014).

Academic librarians are engaging the academic community in research partnerships and formulating new services and policies that capitalize on technological advances that can bridge the academy during this time of growth in the Open Access movement by supporting new digital scholarly communication services. Digital scholarship services include policy development, instruction, the creation of tools and digital research collections, and publishing services that support the wider mission of higher education and the democratization of access through open scholarly publishing.

Policy Development and Instruction

Academic libraries are working to support the academic community during this time of rapid change to the scholarly communication system. This new role in libraries involves not only instruction, collection building, and tool creation, but also advocacy and policy development and implementation for providing leadership to researchers, scholars, teachers, administrators, and the public. Policy development supports institutional discussions, plans, and practices that address the federal requirements for sustainable public access practices, Open Access publishing, and building digital research collections.

New library positions and digital scholarship centers are emerging in order for librarians to partner with disciplinary faculty members across the academy to provide services that support learning and engagement in the research cycle with students and faculty. Some institutions have created copyright education programs that provide instruction and resources to address basic U.S. copyright law, use of Creative Commons licenses, author rights management, and negotiation practices with publishing policies and contracts. When authors retain the bulk of their copyrights, they are better able to place their publications in an institutional repository or on their faculty Web site or profile page. Ultimately, these authors are obtaining further dissemination or further reach for their research and engaging in the growing benefits of Open Access.

Librarians in the past followed guidelines of the minimal amount of copyright-protected work that was permissible to reproduce; for example, the idea that one book chapter could be copied and distributed in a class. Such guidelines were created to avoid copyright infringement, but are not part of the U.S. copyright law. Libraries and other nonprofit organizations both advocate and develop services for possible creation and wide dissemination through the fair use exemption within the U.S. copyright law. Librarians are growing more aware of the demands of copyright law, but even more important is a growing recognition that the conversation should be focused on how librarians can apply fair use factors for educational use and leverage the protective balance that the U.S. Supreme Court intended.

Librarians are uniquely positioned to share their expertise, and they are doing so by offering course instruction, workshops, and individual consultations that support the academy and the changing publishing landscape. Services include several modes of instruction about copyright, intellectual property rights, publishing policies, and author rights management. Other services include course instruction, lectures, hands-on workshops, online resource guides, consultations, and related policy development. The large-scale digital projects require project management, which benefits from the development of memoranda of understanding (MOUs) between the libraries and various campus and community partners. The MOU articulates the responsibilities and duties of each partner, including financial obligations, timeline, rights management and data ownership statement, copyright ownership, and recognition of ongoing maintenance, assessment, and communication reviews.

Collections and Tool Creation

The creation of tools and digital research collections relies on cross-collaborative teamwork within the library and across the academy to manage large-scale, long-term projects that include digitization efforts for analog materials. For example, in the humanities, many special collections departments are digitizing their unique collections to create a corpus for scholars to answer research questions. Such research collection creation calls for tools that contribute to new models of publishing. Widely disseminating scholarship collections involves vendor-created software or open source software.

Tools may provide a new methodology for digital research or assist in making scholarly work more discoverable on the open Web. Library computing services focus on the larger infrastructure and the required hardware, software, and servers to accomplish these growing digital scholarship services. Academic librarians are working to connect software platforms to provide a seamless experience for the user. This type of creation requires addressing the wider infrastructure as well as programming to connect and develop new tools.

Researchers are engaging in emerging forms of digital scholarship. When articles are free to read and free to reuse, Open Access leads to new methodologies and analyses with digital scholarship. When both of these factors are present, librarians and other scholars can build new tools to interact with the articles and uncover new relationships. A search across vast amounts of literature for phrases or concepts can be done more easily and provides the opportunity to compare or analyze a collection of scholarly work. Repositories reflect the distinct collections of a community and give rise to new research opportunities.

MULTITYPE LIBRARY COLLABORATION

Public, school, and special libraries may collaborate with academic libraries to promote publishing in their communities. Libraries are evolving, and as academic libraries reshape their organizations to support the work of scholarly communications, organizational change must occur in order to support new day-to-day operations.

Educating to Create and Publish OERs

New services require staff training, and this need for continuing education across multitype libraries can inspire collaboration. At state library association conferences professional development sessions can be created to bring together multitype libraries. An example is the 2016 Tech Creation and Publishing Institute, a preconference session at the Texas Library Association that addressed publishing and hands-on training with software and social media tools needed to create OERs. This session encouraged those working in a variety of libraries to create OERs and disseminate those learning tools as digital creations through the Research Commons, the repository at the University of Texas at Arlington.

Translating and Publishing Family Stories

Wanting to publish local content in their communities, some libraries find they have limited resources to take on a dynamic community project, so they join together with other libraries. The Stories to Our Children program is an example of a public library partnering with a school district library to promote literacy and community, and to capture family storytelling among Latino families. As students interview their elders, they learn how and when their families came to their city.

This multilibrary collaborative publishing venture is a dynamic example of meaningful engagement in an urban city. Children wrote their stories and university students enrolled in the University of Texas at Arlington's Modern Languages Department provided tutoring support for grammar usage in the native language and translated the stories into English for their college course (Visnak 2015). The libraries brought their communities together with a finished book and a reception on the university campus. The book of stories was compiled, added to the libraries' shelves, and given to each child. This collaborative publishing project gave the authors a powerful experience when they held their family story in a bound book.

The academic librarians have now joined the group and are considering ways to print the book with an inexpensive binding to reduce costs. As they explore possible financing for the ongoing program, they may choose to go with a self-publishing print-on-demand company (mentioned earlier in this book); however, as the need grows, there is interest in pursuing the purchase of an Espresso Book Machine in the future.

Project Gutenberg Self-Publishing Press

The U.S. Declaration of Independence became the first e-text item in 1971 as Project Gutenberg was launched long before computers and the Internet became a household convenience. Project Gutenberg, founded by Michael Hart, encourages free reproduction and distribution of literary material, including e-books. Project Gutenberg has grown to encompass Project Gutenberg Self-Publishing Press, which makes contemporary books and poetry available online and free of charge (http://www.gutenberg.us). This project makes publicly accessible a variety of e-books, images, and texts that are either in the public domain or are still copyrighted and made available with permission from the World Public Library or other consortia provider members. The usage terms and conditions are noted in the header of the file, and users are asked to agree to specific conditions of use that exclude use for commercial purpose without permission. In August 2015 Project Gutenberg celebrated 50,000 items (Cook 2015).

Open Textbook Initiatives Provide an Alternative to College Costs

The Open Textbook Network (OTN) aims to support a network of academic institutions with open textbook initiatives. The OTN stems from the University of Minnesota's Center for Open Education, supports network members who want to adopt open textbooks for the classroom, and simultaneously is building the Open Textbook Library of peer-reviewed open textbooks. The OTN trainers work with university faculty and have experienced a 40 percent open textbook adoption rate as a result of their faculty education and engagement strategies (University of Minnesota 2015). This is an emerging way for community colleges and other institutions that are working toward solutions for the high cost of textbooks. The open textbooks are written and reviewed by faculty and written for college faculty to use. Open textbooks are beginning to have an impact on the high costs associated with textbooks. For example, a statistics book may cost $180, although the open textbook is free and may cost the student $20–$40 dollars to print. This price differential is especially meaningful for the majority of college students who worry about their grades and still don't purchase textbooks due to high textbook costs.

IMPLICATIONS FOR THE FUTURE

The ongoing evolution in the open movement is accelerating Open Access, Open Education, and Open Government and has led to a convergence in Open Access, Open Data, and OERs with implications for libraries. As libraries populate repositories, create collections and digital tools, and create policy and procedures that support openness, they are entering a dynamic and interconnected world where scholarly partnerships in research and publishing will become the norm. The dissemination and storage of the university's scholarly output will be valuable for new types of digital research analysis, the reuse of research data, and an increased network of rich digital research content.

The nature of scholarly communications work will continue to foster wider readership as well as research partnerships among librarians, their faculty, researchers, students, and community members. Librarians are well positioned to support access and reuse of materials that traditionally have been less available for dissemination. These materials include publications that fulfill a niche in a faculty's area of expertise. Among other digital publishing services, libraries could also provide a print-on-demand publishing service center and connect community members from school and public libraries to those in the academy in new and innovative ways.

Libraries are increasingly agents of change in the creation and dissemination functions diffusing new knowledge into our digital lives. The work being done will have long-term results as libraries continue shifting priorities to meet the demands of writers, authors, and readers in our society. After all, the end goal is to bring institutional repositories together into a wider network of open scholarship and publications and to democratize access while providing storage and preservation, giving every citizen the opportunity to learn and innovate beyond the walls of the academy and into larger public spaces.

CHAPTER SUMMARY

Academic libraries have a tradition of providing a variety of services for their higher education community. As the scholarly communication system continues to change in our increasingly digital world, libraries are building Open Access services aimed at meeting the evolving digital scholarship needs of the researchers, faculty, students, staff, and administrators on their campus. This time of transition in Open Access scholarly publishing is an opportunity for librarians to recognize the changing publishing environment and take up the call to be proactive and innovate solutions.

Librarians can be a bridge to providing new services and tools that support Open Access and wider dissemination of scholarly and creative endeavors that will enhance the academic and professional success of faculty and students. In order for such innovations to arise, librarians will participate in the scholarly communication system through their work and will continue to learn about scholarly communication issues and best practices. Academic libraries are finding a niche in the "Library as Publisher" paradigm and developing a whole suite of digital publishing and digital scholarship services that include publishing, author rights management education, the creation of collections, and increased engagement with the local community through partnerships.

The publishing industry is not alone in the call for innovative solutions. Librarians are well positioned to provide unique expertise that brings together the elements of creation, dissemination, storage, and preservation that builds upon digital publishing solutions while supporting the academy's need to make accessible current research and creative endeavors.

Consider the intended audience and how they are likely to access your work, then consider weighing publishing and distribution options. Open Access publishing alternatives may just make sense.

REFERENCES

Association of Research Libraries. 2012. *SPARC Open Access Newsletter and Forum*. http://www.sparc.arl.org/news/sparc-open-access-newsletter-forum. Accessed December 28, 2015.

Cook, Michael. 2015. "Project Gutenberg Releases eBook, #50,000." *Project Gutenberg News*, October 3. http://www.gutenbergnews.org/20151003/project-gutenberg-releases-ebook-50000. Accessed October 8, 2015.

Crawford, Walt. 2011. *Open Access: What You Need to Know*. Chicago: American Library Association.

CrossRef. 2015. http://www.crossref.org/#.

Lippincott, Joan K., Harriette Hemmasi, and Vivian Marie Lewis. 2014. "Trends in Digital Scholarship Centers." *EDUCAUSE Review Online*, June 16. http://er.educause.edu/articles/2014/6/trends-in-digital-scholarship-centers. Accessed December 3, 2015.

OASIS. 2015. Open Access Scholarly Information Sourcebook. http://www.openoasis.org. Accessed November 19, 2015.

Open Journal of Astrophysics. 2016. Cornell University Library. http://arxiv.org/archive/astro-ph. Accessed January 9, 2016.

Price, Kenneth M., and Ed Folsom, eds. 2015. The Walt Whitman Archive. http://whitmanarchive.org. Accessed December 28, 2015.

SPARC. 2015. Scholarly Publishing and Academic Resources Coalition. http://www.sparc.arl.org/about#sthash.vZMWkeqY.dpuf. Accessed November 2, 2015.

University of Minnesota. 2015. Open Textbook Network. http://research.cehd.umn.edu/open/open-textbook-network. Accessed January 9, 2016.

Visnak, Kelly. 2015. Interview with Professor Alicia Rueda-Acedo. University of Texas at Arlington, November 2, 2015.

ISSUES AND RESOURCES

CHAPTER OVERVIEW

This final chapter summarizes major ideas from previous chapters and presents an annotated listing of recommended books and Internet resources on various aspects of self-publishing. This chapter highlights writing and publishing trends featuring a partnership between librarians and writers.

MAJOR CONCEPTS

Since our world is rapidly changing, publishing also is experiencing cataclysmic change, providing the opportunity for librarians and writers to engage in a creative and productive partnership in this transformational setting. This book is devoted to the evolution of traditional publishing and library service, and the challenges associated with writing and publishing in a digital age. Technology advances have spawned the Open Access movement and have prompted a revolution in publishing and the role of libraries in their support of writers as they conduct research, write, edit, design, and publish their work.

Following are major concepts outlined in this book:

The Information Transfer Model Provides a Framework for Thinking about Publishing

The information transfer cycle represents the life cycle for information in any format. It is helpful to consider this model, defined in Chapter 1, when thinking about publishing and the role of librarians, information professionals, and authors in the publishing process. Individuals considering self-publication will find the model helpful for understanding the many aspects of publication beyond the writing process.

Applying the information transfer model, we define "publishing" as the creation, recording, reproduction, and dissemination of information—processes that have changed substantially because of advances in technology. Librarians should be knowledgeable about the publishing processes and resources available to help their clientele self-publish.

Librarians and Libraries Are Engaging with Their Communities

Prior to the maker movement, libraries typically offered customers story time programs and special events in addition to research opportunities in genealogy and various courses in computer word processing and spreadsheet mastery. Introductory "how to" sessions in e-mail and social media were common. With an emphasis on technology, libraries often also provide computer, tablet, and gadget troubleshooting and training.

With a learning commons theme, today's libraries support more than searching and completing online applications and resumes. Some libraries have ventured into the realms of cookery, crafts, recreation, Lego and robot building, 3D printing, and print-on-demand publishing. Libraries partnering with other organizations, government agencies, or corporations is a more recent development that integrates libraries with their communities.

Technology Has Revolutionized Publishing

The computer, word processing, the Internet, laser printers, sophisticated software, and printing technology have changed how we think about publishing. As communication changed with improvements in technology, information transfer was expedited. Development of computers and telecommunications technologies transcended barriers of time and space, creating a participatory culture in which information consumers also have become information producers. In this digital age, a time of continuous and massive change, librarians have the knowledge and skills to engage with writers who want to self-publish their work. Now is the time to initiate this winning partnership.

Writing Requires Creative Planning

Writing is a creative process, and the thought processes involved in planning a book are the same, whether for self-publishing or for submission to a commercial publisher. A publisher provides valuable expertise in the editing, design, indexing, printing, distribution, and marketing of a book—processes that must be addressed by an author when self-publishing.

Planning early in the process is important for an author. Using the elements of a typical book proposal serves as an outline for the author to follow and encourages the author to consider the intended audience and marketing. The intended audience, while valuable for marketing, is an essential ingredient in the decision-making process as the author is writing.

Attempts to Publish Commercially Often End in Rejection

An author must decide whether to submit a proposal or manuscript for commercial publishing or pursue self-publishing. Submitting to a commercial publisher is a time-consuming process that often ends in rejection. Access to new technology now gives writers the opportunity to assume roles that publishers traditionally have filled. Investing that time into improving your manuscript may be more rewarding.

The Stigma of Self-Publishing Is Dissipating

Self-publishing is often equated with poor-quality work and is seen as a last resort for authors who are unable to publish their work through traditional channels, but that stigma is being challenged by highly successful work published independently and marketed directly to readers. Self-publishing served Jane Austen, Walt Whitman, Virginia Woolf, Marcel Proust, Ursula Le Guin, Joan Aiken, Kij Johnson, Karen Joy Fowler, and numerous other authors well and can serve other writers well.

Self-Publishing Is a Small Business Venture

Writing a book is something many people want to do, but writing the book and seeing it published are time-consuming, laborious tasks. A publisher provides valuable expertise in the editing, design, indexing, printing, distribution, and marketing of a book—processes that an author assumes when self-publishing. In other words, the self-publishing author is the CEO of her own small business.

Publishing Is a Rapidly Changing Business Model

The process of publishing a book and getting it into readers' hands is a rapidly shifting model that is affecting change for writers, publishers, libraries, and readers. Self-publishing is more affordable and accessible than ever before, and many writers are eliminating the middleman and submitting their work for reader approval through the open market. Savvy companies are competing with the self-publishing boom by offering writers new programs and platforms for printing and sharing their work. Profit models, contract terms, and licensing options are evolving.

Librarians Can Partner Effectively with Writers to Self-Publish

Librarians are perfectly positioned to guide and support writers in their communities as they seek information and make important decisions about publishing their work. Partnering with writers to give them the skills to sort through the myriad services and avenues for self-publication is an extension of reference services to the writers in their communities, and it also empowers librarians. Seeking the most accurate information and comparing potential routes for self-publishing is a perfect way to gain the insight necessary to stay current and contribute knowledgeably to the professional discussion on self-publishing.

As librarians determine the best way to adapt library services and thrive in the midst of this chaotic information age, they have an opportunity to guide the changes and craft solutions that will work for everyone involved.

Internet-Based Resources and Social Media Can Support Self-Publishing

Social media have entered the mainstream and can be used to promote self-published books and other publications. Librarians can create and support a culture of reading and writing through creative use of new technologies and social media. Subscription-based and freely available Web 2.0 features can provide writers with LibGuides and pathfinders as writers conduct research for their works, and these finding aids can promote authors' books. Additionally, librarians can partner with writers to utilize social media, publication and presentation software, and other recent developments in technology to promote self-published books.

Creating Author Communities Is a Core Author Support Service

Connecting writers to one another is as core to the library profession and what libraries stand for as connecting people to print or digital library resources. The library can support authors with resources, programming, and encouragement, and one of the most important things that libraries can provide writers is the opportunity to connect to other writers and readers in a friendly and encouraging space. Building a community of writers and increasing access to self-publishing resources helps shift the perception of the library from a passive repository of materials to an active ally for self-published authors.

Author Support Services Must Align with a Library's Mission

Promoting self-publishing and supporting writers through library services is easier in theory than in practice. Serving writers through public programming creates challenges unique to each institution because libraries vary in size, service area, funding, staffing, and service goals. Every library is unique, and the programming offered should align with the mission of the library and the needs and wants of the community. Additionally, librarians must curate quality public events while empowering emerging authors with equal access to events and resources, which can pit one core value of the profession against another. Finding the right strategy will likely be a process of trial and error, and librarians must be willing to experiment, fail, evaluate, and try again.

A Successful Writing Program Focuses on Skills Building and Community Engagement

Rather than hosting contests that create winners, losers, and competition within a writing community, librarians can help everyone who is interested learn more about the craft of writing, self-publishing options, and the business of being a writer. Libraries that support writers in skill development and marketing success can become the hub of a thriving writing community and an integral piece of the literary culture of their communities.

The Open Access Movement Contributes to the Shift in the Publishing Paradigm

Open Access brings a new paradigm—a new value system and approach to publishing. The Open Access movement draws libraries and information professionals into research and publishing in new ways. The Open Access movement has encouraged rethinking and restructuring of the research and publishing processes. As the access to information becomes more readily available, so does the opportunity to be an author. An evolution is underway in which the opportunity to discover, learn, discuss, create, and disseminate digital work is stimulating an evolution in publishing—an evolution made possible by the open movement. Academic libraries have provided leadership in this movement, leveraging partnerships and opportunities for collaboration with other types of libraries and their communities.

Librarians Must Be Assertive in Promoting Their Services

Before listing suggested resources for librarians and writers, we offer this final thought. Libraries are a vital resource in most communities, yet writers may overlook this valuable resource and the librarians who provide the services. We close with the stark realization brought to us by a Kansas author, Steve A. Anderson, who told us after his first effort to publish, "I wish I knew librarians could have helped me in my process!"

Librarians must be assertive in their communities to make known that we have few self-published writers like Steve, who were unaware of the support available in their local library!

RELATED RESOURCES: BOOKS

Librarians can assist clientele with a vast collection of traditional print materials and electronic resources. Although numerous books have been published guiding writers through the publishing process, this list includes Web sites, books, and other resources that have been frequently utilized.

Crawford, Walt. 2012. *The Librarian's Guide to Micropublishing: Helping Patrons and Communities Use Free and Low-Cost Publishing Tools to Tell Their Stories*. **Medford, NJ: Information Today.**

This handbook helps patrons tell their stories by taking advantage of free or low-cost publication tools. Crawford's manual directs librarians who wish to steer writers on the publishing path. Whether a client desires a few copies of a genealogy report for a family reunion or hundreds of copies of a policy document for employees, these step-by-step instructions help librarians and authors design and edit manuscripts. Recommendations include selecting cost-effective, practical templates; avoiding expensive photographs, charts, and illustrations; and knowing what to outsource and what to personally complete. Comparisons of Lulu, CreateSpace, and other digital instruments equip librarians to guide their clientele in the production of quality print books.

DiLeo, Jeffrey R. 2014. *Turning the Page: Book Culture in the Digital Age—Essays, Reflections, Interventions*. **Huntsville, TX: Texas Review Press.**

Technological innovations in the current century have evolved into various forms of print media. Reading through the lens of blogs, Web sites, e-books, and social media has not only become common, it has altered opportunities in the printing and publishing world. Electronic dissemination allows information to be transferred any time, any place. The philosophy of "just in time" is apparent today with "green books" available electronically with the click of a mouse or an icon. This historical snapshot reflects the goals of publication assisting librarians and their clientele in reviewing the culture of books and the prospect of technology trends.

Germano, William. 2008. *Getting It Published: A Guide for Scholars and Anyone Else Serious about Serious Books*. **2nd ed. Chicago and London: University of Chicago Press.**

In a competitive and confusing publishing world, Germano defines the types and tasks of the publisher, editor, designer, publicist, and illustrator. Ranging from creating a proposal to avoiding mistakes, this academic guide suggests how librarians and authors can pitch their manuscripts and circumvent publishing quagmires. The mysteries of traditional print and self-publishing are unveiled in this manual.

Hushion, Bill, and Peter Wright. 2007. *Self-Publishing: An Insider's Guide*. **Mississauga, ON: Guerilla Gourmet.**

Although this book was published in 2007, it remains a reliable resource complete with the elements of publishing. Since a writer may not understand certain responsibilities, this manual provides a sequence guiding authors through the process of securing an ISBN number, barcode number, quote, cover designer, printer, and marketing strategy. Descriptions of the roles each professional plays will save the writer time and assuage any anxiety. Suggestions include selecting a classification or genre for identification and promotional purposes that highlights the book's features and attracts select audiences. Knowing what is unique about the book aids in the development of the promotional approach. Understanding each piece of the puzzle and the timing of the process can greatly impact sales. Following Hushion and Wright's plan will support any writer's vision of becoming published.

Kawasaki, Guy, and Shawn Welch. 2013. *APE: Author, Publisher, Entrepreneur—How to Publish a Book*. Palo Alto, CA: Nononina Press.

The authors insist that the days of "vanity presses" and traditional publishing are gone, and new advances in technology enable writers to publish their own works. Kawasaki and Welch examine the processes of traditional publishing and reveal the age of entrepreneurial writers who assume the roles previously occupied by publishing companies. This guide to self-publishing suggests numerous tools to help the enterprising writer and provides solid advice for achieving a quality publication.

Lupton, Ellen, ed. 2008. *Indie Publishing: How to Design and Produce Your Own Book*. New York: Princeton Architectural Press.

Self-publishing, among other topics, is included in this manual with a "nuts and bolts" guide to creating and distributing. Filled with publishing essentials, traditional techniques, informative infographics, flowcharts, and marketing strategies, this book's clear illustrations and concise instructions explore basic design and printing principles. The handmade book chapter focuses on do-it-yourself procedures promoting a makerspace movement in a learning commons era. Lupton defines the multiple roles of a self-publisher including editor, financier, marketer, distributor, and more.

Price, Lynn. 2010. *The Writer's Essential Tackle Box: Getting a Hook on the Publishing Industry*. Lake Forest, CA: Behler Publications.

Incorporating a tackle box metaphor, the author Lynn Price guides writers who are "fishing" for agents, editors, and publishers. Skim through the questions and locate the section that will be most beneficial, or read the entire book cover to cover unpacking all the interesting questions an author should ask before signing a contract. A variety of sources, a survival guide, and tricks of trade publishing and self-publishing are included. The author's blog and Web site provide current trends and updates at http://behlerblog.com. A comical, animated book description can be viewed at http://www.behlerpublications.com/titles-price-tackle.shtml.

Shillingsburg, Peter L. 2006. *From Gutenberg to Google: Electronic Representations of Literary Texts*. Cambridge: Cambridge University Press.

This historical perspective of the manuscript to press continuum considers the trials and tribulations of printing over the years and traces the writing and publishing processes. Transferring texts from handwritten copy to print to electronic formats are explored. The changes in composition, editing, production, dissemination, and archiving are revealed. Celebrate achievements in technological accuracy and caution potential consequences of electronic publishing. Shillingsburg examines the current state of publishing in contrast to traditional methods.

Smallwood, Carol, ed. 2010. *Writing and Publishing: The Librarian's Handbook.* **Chicago, IL: American Library Association.**

Since librarians frequently package information in a variety of formats, this book is targeted for librarians who wish to publish. Typically librarians design and distribute book reviews, flyers, newsletters, brochures, and press releases for informational or promotional purposes. Whether attending civic meetings, presenting at conferences, offering staff training, or providing professional development, librarians will value this manual complete with strategies and realistic examples of marketing and publishing their programs and events.

Thompsett-Scott, Beth, ed. 2014. *Marketing with Social Media: A Library and Information Technology Association Guide.* **Chicago, IL: American Library Association.**

These contributors offer innovative techniques for effective marketing guiding librarians who are assisting their clientele with social media. With examples from different library types and locations, these recommendations include promising examples of Facebook, wikis, video-sharing sites, Pinterest, Google+, Foursquare, blogs, Twitter, and QR codes. Utilizing a variety of resources, this guide features screen shots, illustrations, and planning tactics for librarians and practitioners who wish to brand their messages to foster conversation and improve connections.

Weber, Steve. 2011. *ePublish: Self-Publish Fast and Profitably for Kindle, CreateSpace, iPhone and Print on Demand.* **Stephen A. Weber.**

With a "communities trump companies" mindset, Steve Weber presents successful self-publishing scenarios guiding writers through a potential publishing quagmire. Authors will benefit from Weber's vast experiences, saving valuable time and resources. Readers of the manual can take advantage of recommended apps and features; for instance, the Kindle free formatting tutorials train writers in how to submit their work in a reader-friendly layout. Gain the expertise of complimentary beta readers by submitting an excerpt or chapter for others to read and comment. Weber recommends utilizing Many Books (http://manybooks .net) to read more than 33,000 free books on a Kindle, Nook, iPad, and other devices. Numerous electronic examples instruct writers in how to avoid pitfalls and increase publishing opportunities.

LIBRARIANS SUPPORTING WRITERS

Librarians collaborating with authors can utilize a wealth of resources. With the availability of digital tracking, analytics can assist librarians as they diagnose and recommend the treatment that will best serve as a course of action. Online tutorials help and may assuage some anxiety writers experience along the road to publication. Librarians can inform their clientele of the enhanced features and functionality of the recommended resources beyond online help discussions. With combined interests and information, librarians and authors can access numerous experts for guidance.

Resource guides and "Put It in Writing @ Your Library" workshops sponsored by the American Library Association are examples of resources for aspiring writers. Librarians can glean tips for hosting a writing workshop and educate and entertain clientele with successful scenarios. Visit http://www.ala.org/advocacy/advleg/publicawareness/campaign@your library/sponsorship/hostwritersworkshop for details.

Libraries support the vision of lifelong learning and inspire "the art of the story" as witnessed across the nation. For example, the Story Center (http://www.mymcpl.org/events /story-center-series) offers materials, resources, and opportunities for showcasing oral, print, and digital stories. Members can collaborate with writers and librarians accessing indoor and outdoor experiences in their knowledge quest with an amazing gallery of opportunities.

Bridging the gap between those with and those without access to information may plague the literacy community; nonetheless, librarians will persist as they continue to raise awareness about the plethora of resources available to every client. Libraries Transform, an initiative of ALA (http://www.ilovelibraries.org/librariestransform/about), is designed to shed light on the impact of libraries and the numerous services provided. This energetic voice showcases "the transformative nature of today's libraries and elevating the critical role libraries play in the digital age."

Similar to the New Hanover County Public Library's vision, located at http://libguides .nhclibrary.org/future, librarians have been reaching and connecting with community members and will continue to incorporate technological advances, collaborating on programs and events embracing this paradigm shift into new reading, researching, and publishing endeavors beyond traditional printing.

In an *Atlantic Monthly* issue, the article "How Genius Works" connects cultures inside the imaginative minds of accomplished authors and artists, demonstrating how they have discovered their creative flair (http://www.theatlantic.com/special-report/how-genius-works). Likewise, librarians have ignited and guided their patrons who are expressing themselves by providing opportunities to share and publish their passions.

ONLINE PUBLISHING SOURCES

Information professionals collaborating with clientele in research, writing, revision, and publishing ventures may benefit from these suggested online resources. Identifying the features worthy of promotion and reaching the desired audience remains an essential element throughout the publishing process.

Archway Publishing (http://www.archwaypublishing.com)

A division of Simon & Schuster, Archway Publishing provides a range of unique packages for children and adult fiction, nonfiction, and business writers. Similar to a librarian, a concierge leads the author through the entire self-publishing process ranging from book design to colorful features with print, electronic, and audio formats. With layout, production, publicity, and bookselling services, the tailored bundle directs subscribers through a practical route. Publishers typically offer a gatekeeper to assist and track the process similar to a librarian serving patrons.

The Book Designer (http://www.thebookdesigner.com)

Preventing pitfalls is the key to this guide comparing previous self-publishing practices to current self-publishing trends. Avoid costly and time-consuming mistakes by following Joel Friedlander's "10 Things You Need to Know about Self-Publishing." Librarians can assist writers by reviewing their options and expectations including finance and photography. Develop a business plan, since the author also becomes the editor, publisher, and much more. Descriptions of subsidy publishers and nonembeddable fonts coach authors with simple keys along the self-publishing journey.

Book Launch Toolkit (http://authortoolkits.com/booklaunchtoolkit)

For purchase, the Book Launch Toolkit offers simple procedures to "launch your writing career" and boasts a platform to assist authors. Select the appropriate package and utilize the templates and media launch pad to build a writing platform. Take advantage of book trailers and promotional bundles for support.

BookWorks: The Self-Publishers Association
(https://www.bookworks.com)

Self-publishers unite and share publishing and promotional resources at BookWorks. Locate editors and designers assisting writers along the publishing path. By joining this community, librarians and writers can access blogs, interact with other writers, and showcase their work. Learn how to compose book cover and advertising blurbs promoting your manuscript. Additional services and experts are available for subscription fees.

CreateSpace (https://www.createspace.com)

Utilize CreateSpace's free publishing resources to compose content, format files, market your work, and access additional tips and tricks. Efficiently access tools, booksellers, and e-book delivery options attracting your audience.

IndyPublish (http://www.indypublish.com)

IndyPublish is an online toolkit complete with advice, tools, and industry links. Chat with others via the Interact Café. Independent authors can polish and publish with this affordable and flexible company. Take advantage of their global distribution marketplace giving authors the infrastructure of paper and electronic formats to store and sell their manuscripts. Indy boasts writing tools, professionally bound covers, and other features.

iUniverse (http://www.iuniverse.com)

"Publish your book, your way" with iUniverse, an editorial, marketing, and publishing service with global distribution opportunities. Guided by format, design, and promotional professionals, writers have access to a plethora of experts and resources.

Lightning Source (https://www.lightningsource.com)

Follow the prescribed Lightning Source flowchart: secure a publisher via their digital library, distribute materials to book buyers, utilize global delivery channels, ship to prospective book buyers globally, and connect to customers. Intended for independent, medium-sized, and large publishers, this print-on-demand service offers a cover and file template generator, layout and color suggestions, binding features, design support, marketing strategies, and submission techniques. This online tool boasts efficient and quality printing and distribution networking.

Matador (http://www.troubador.co.uk/matador.asp)

If you are interested in an overseas self-publishing partner in the United Kingdom, Matador guides writers through writing, editing, ISBN registration, cover design, printing, and marketing. Publishing e-books is also an option. Whether your goal is to publish a cookbook, family tree, or a collection of poetry, Matador's workshops, podcasts, and staff will steer you in the right direction. Trade and social media marketing and distribution services are available to established and aspiring authors internationally. Good if a writer wants to break into a European market.

Scribd (https://www.scribd.com)

Read and listen to books and submit your works to this self-publishing company. Enjoy your personal digital library via this subscription service with 80 million global readers. Take advantage of unique features including a conversion technology allowing manuscripts to be read on any device.

SELF-e Powered by Library Journal (http://self-e.libraryjournal.com)

Engage your local writing community with SELF-e, a novel approach encouraging authors and librarians to collaborate on submissions that transform into e-books. Embrace the digital age with this efficient process making e-books available to readers from local writers. Distribute self-published e-books into public libraries at no cost via SELF-e. Librarians can request complimentary trials to learn more about this resource for authors and readers.

Smashwords (https://www.smashwords.com)

Make e-book self-publishing efficient with Smashwords by submitting your online manuscript. Upload your book at no cost and follow the guidelines accepting narratives in simple text formats with this popular tool. Authors and librarians should not experience anxiety and may be comforted with the clear and concise procedures.

Woodneath Press (http://www.mymcpl.org)

Take advantage of the print-on-demand features of the Espresso Book Machine. Publish novels, anthologies, cookbooks, scrapbooks, and journals. Share accomplishments and resources. Events include author fairs, poetry slams, book clubs, story time, reading programs, and writing workshops.

Writer's Digest (http://www.writersdigest.com)

Although Writer's Digest provides roadmaps, there are no rules. Creating a blog and other social media forms are encouraged. Librarians can assist clientele writing a short story, children's book, collection of poetry or stories, or a fiction or nonfiction book with these guidelines. By customizing a blog, authors can self-promote, build an audience, and make connections. Tips cover basic online writing principles, understanding the reader, and knowing the market. Librarians can offer workshops focusing on a writing genre or style, an element such as characterization, voice, or plot, in addition to a publishing goal.

The Write Life (http://thewritelife.com)

The Write Life recognizes the facets of publishing a book; therefore, a flowchart was designed to provide authors with the decision-making skills to determine whether to self-publish or pursue traditional publishing. An infographic allows writers to ponder their purpose and choose a publishing path. A Write Life feature identifies the 100 best Web sites for writers at http://thewritelife.com/100-best-websites-for-writers-2014/#.no3i2iy:Uqi.

WRITING WORKSHOPS

This section highlights writing services that can be made available to patrons at libraries or online. Some librarians have provided their clientele with creative learning opportunities by hosting events intended to spur the imagination and appeal to established and would-be authors. Glean from a few prime successful samples.

Chapbooks

Chapbooks can ignite and inspire conversation, creativity, and give clientele the support and encouragement to express themselves. Librarians can use chapbooks as an icebreaker, sentence starter, or community-created program that can be inexpensive in paper or electronic forms.

Designed to brainstorm ideas and prompt writing, a chapbook is a booklet or pamphlet published digitally or in traditional paper format. "From the 16th to the 19th century, chapbooks flourished as a locus of popular culture, religion, folklore, myth, history, poetry, and story" (Gordon 2007). Chapbooks were originally crafted by hand or cheaply printed in Europe and Asia during this time and possibly dispersed by chapmen. Later in America, chapbooks were popular among American Beat poets during the 1950s and 1960s who had limited accessibility and funds for printing.

No specific formula dictates a chapbook's layout; however, this small book may be an inspirational notebook for ballads, tales, poetry, songs, short stories, and drawings. Although chapbooks are found on college campuses, they serve a purpose in public and school libraries generating creativity. Librarians can liberate writers with thought-provoking examples fostering publishing with this do-it-yourself guide.

Typically limited to one poem, drawing, or song per page, a chapbook may consist of a wide range of styles, forms, expressions, and aesthetics and may be self-published, handmade, or printed in limited quantities. Style distinguishes chapbooks from other publications. Guidelines and samples are located at http://anabiosispress.org/chapguides.html and http://www.pw.org/content/diy_how_to_make_and_bind_chapbooks?cmnt_all=1.

Academic, Community, Public, and Special-Interest Libraries

Community colleges, technical colleges, and universities typically house libraries with unique features intended to captivate students and professors. Traditional and technology-rich scavenger hunts and videos engage and entertain today's adult learners. To access their continued educational opportunities, training and supporting research, writing, and the publishing process, locate academic libraries in your area. Visit local, state, and national libraries in order to glean from their professional expertise in traditional pathfinders, Lib-Guides, tutorials, and electronic publishing ventures. Public, historical, and specialized libraries, and museums provide human contact and online databases with a plethora of resources. Access information professionals at a variety of academic institutions and take advantage of the available sessions, events, and programs.

Badgerdog Creative Writing Workshops (http://www.austinlibrary.org)

Badgerdog Creative Writing workshops are typically offered for three weeks for 3rd-through 12th-grade students. Student writers work closely with a professional writer exploring poetry, fiction, nonfiction, and playwriting. Students experience performing and publishing their work. Comic book writing workshops are also available.

Adults are welcome to participate in Austin (Texas) libraries and community centers. Writers' fiction, poetry, or nonfiction work is printed in a chapbook. Librarians and clientele are united in a common quest to compose and create stories. Samples can be viewed at http://www.austinlibrary.org/site/PageServer?pagename=bdog_what.

Elementia (http://jocolibrary.org/teens/elementia)

Johnson County (Kansas) Public Libraries (JCPL) encourage teen participation in *Elementia*, a collection of young adult original fiction, nonfiction, poetry, graphic stories, art, and photography. JCPL provide patrons with access to materials and experiences that enrich their lives with access to tools and equipment. The JCPL Makerspace movement incorporates publishing programs serving the Kansas City area. Librarians Kate McNair and Angel Jewel Tucker were featured in *The Library as Incubator Project* on Elementia at http://www.libraryasincubatorproject.org/?p=16921. Their success (http://kcur.org/post/how-johnson-county-librarians-grow-young-poets) has attracted numerous authors and artists to inspire their youth for more than a decade.

Flow Tactics Teen Poetry Workshop (http://reallifepoets.org)

Flow Tactics is a poetry workshop for middle- and high school–age teens at the Birmingham (Alabama) Public Library. The workshop is led by Real Life Poets, a nonprofit creative writing group whose purpose is "Changing minds, one rhyme at a time!" Writing and open microphone events focus on patron interests and desires to continue writing. Librarians can glean from their experiences while assisting their clientele to write, publish, and promote their works.

New Hanover County Public Library Writer's Workshop (http://libguides.nhclibrary.org/c.php?g=256048&p=1709558)

With branches in Wilmington and Carolina Beach (North Carolina), the New Hanover County Public Library gives patrons access to a wealth of resources and professional guidance. Utilize the composing, editing, and publication tools. The Multimedia Lab provides an opportunity for script writing for those patrons who prefer play and film writing at http://libguides.nhclibrary.org/multimedia. Learn the tricks for writing for magazines, news, and various genres and engage in meaningful dialogue with other authors.

Springfield City Library (http://www.springfieldlibrary.org/library
/services/arts-entertainment-programs)

Writing workshops and author fairs are two of the numerous programs featured at the Springfield City (Massachusetts) Library. Beyond keyboard classes and story time, participate in the rich dialogue encompassing music, entertainment, art, reading, writing, and craft sessions.

Write Club (http://www.hooverlibrary.org/services/write-club)

Join the Hoover (Alabama) Write Club to meet and exchange ideas with other authors. Inspire and encourage writers with your literary thoughts in a supportive network filled with constructive criticism and complimentary feedback. Learn how libraries foster reading, authors, and writing in a creative and digital world and celebrate Southern voices.

Writers in the Schools (https://www.lectures.org)

Writers in the Schools inspires teens to discover their true voice. The Seattle (Washington) Public Library and Seattle Arts and Lectures encourage writing and performance arts. Youth develop their talents through chapbooks, letters, songs, biographies, and poetry. Join educators, librarians, and authors to express yourself and showcase your talents.

PUBLISHING SUPPORT TOOLS

Librarians have taken advantage of promotional and publishing tools for decades. Nonetheless, software and online packages have improved, allowing users to create enhanced products. Signage, business cards, bookmarks, brochures, stationery, newsletters, infographics, calendars, registration forms, webpages, and more are available with embedded audible "bells and whistles" to publicize information.

Book Creator for iPad (http://support.redjumper.net/hc/en-us/articles
/201908301-Your-first-book)

Book Creator for iPad is a free program, with an optional less than $5 upgrade, allowing authors to create their own e-books. Books can be started in a portrait, square, or landscape format, and a variety of text and colors enhance the book. Designers can insert photos and sound (from the Internet or their own) on individual pages. An author can make multiple books and organize them into bookshelves.

Constant Contact (http://www.constantcontact.com)

Create professional e-mail newsletters. Explore the features, customize images, insert documents, and embed videos and Web sites. The app has mobile-friendly templates to ensure the publication can be seen from any device. Post and track e-mails on your social networks. Archived newsletters are automatically updated upon revision. Pending your audience and purpose, subscribe for $20–$45 monthly.

Creative Bloq (http://www.creativebloq.com)

Create professional brochures from an amazing gallery of templates and design portfolios for any event. Bring your book to life, astonish your audience, and circulate your publication by following concise steps. Tutorials, videos, and interviews clarify details and provide examples.

Google Drive (https://www.google.com/drive)

Google Drive includes documents, sheets, sites, slides, forms, maps, and apps with business cards, bookmarks, brochures, and booklets. Watch for new resources and frequent updates. Google boasts that users have unlimited storage for files and documents, which can be linked or embedded for electronic distribution. Options include simple templates incorporating tables, calendars, and images. Animated small picture books, project schedulers, diary journal writing, and UJAM music maker are additional features. If revisions need to be made after publishing, the changes will automatically update. Since Google possesses cloud storage, users are not limited to free file space.

Google Drive's programs Lucidchart and Drawings are online creation (or canvas) tools accessible anywhere via a computer or mobile device. Librarians and writers can collaborate on projects with others from a distance. Lucidchart is a program that allows users to create flowcharts and diagrams, for example a family tree or the flow of operations within a business. A variety of shapes and arrows can be color-coded, identifying the order of progression or related items. Images from the Web and links to external Web sites can be inserted. Similar to Microsoft Excel, multiple pages of charts are allowed. Lucidchart has a presentation function as well.

Drawings acts as an online Microsoft Paint program, which allows users to create a slide with clip art or basic shapes from the gallery. Pictures or text from other programs or the Internet can be inserted into the canvas and manipulated alongside other elements. As with Lucidchart or Google Docs, librarians and their clientele can work on a single project together from a distance and exchange comments.

InDesign (https://www.adobe.com/products/indesign.html)

InDesign is desktop publishing software by Adobe Systems for publishing posters, fliers, brochures, magazines, newspapers, and books. The design environment integrates Adobe Photoshop, Illustrator, Acrobat, and Flash Professional. An Android device, iPhone, or iPad can also produce designs. Only limited by your imagination, colorful and creative publications can be disseminated to appropriate audiences. Since InDesign is a part of Adobe Creative Cloud, updates and future releases are automatically available. Licensed InDesign membership is available by subscription.

Microsoft Publisher (http://www.microsoftstore.com/store/msusa/en _US/pdp/Publisher-2016/productID.323025400)

This program is user-friendly and available at low or no cost. Promotional items can be made using templates or by starting from a blank document. Templates can also be suited to organizational color themes or to incorporate logos. Each newsletter starts with four pages and more pages can be added as necessary. Each document has rulers and guidelines to properly align content. Calendars, signup sheets, and order or response forms can be inserted. Completed newsletters can be sent via e-mail as an attachment to be disseminated to others. Publisher documents cannot be shared via Google Docs at this time.

Additional features include business cards, brochures, stationery, newsletters, and much more. The images, icons, fonts, graphics, and capabilities enhance the final product.

Microsoft Word (http://www.microsoftstore.com/store/msusa/en_US /pdp/Word-2016/productID.323026000?)

Creating a newsletter, brochure, business card, flyer, or bookmark in Microsoft Word is possible but may have limitations. Templates help with the format and design. A user can start with a blank Word document, manipulating elements one by one to achieve the desired appearance. Word has rulers along the top and side but may not have guides on the document to help keep newsletter elements aligned. Once finished, Word documents can easily be sent via e-mail to recipients; however, electronic distributing of newsletters may be limited (at least those created with templates) via Google Docs.

Tackk (https://tackk.com)

Tackk is a sharable content-creating program for newsletters and presentations for school or social networking purposes. The application allows users to link with other social media sites private or publicly. With the flair of Pinterest, Twitter, and Smore, Tackk provides a variety of templates for different projects, or users with a blank canvas choose the colors or color scheme and insert various pieces of content like text, photos, videos, music, and buttons (links to other Web sites). Other options include selling/buying forms, RSVP, and contact forms. Tackks can have personalized URLs, and users can choose to enable a content stream to generate discussion over the content of their Tackks.

CONCLUDING COMMENT

Information professionals can assist writers by offering face-to-face and online seminars and tutorials in evolving publishing ventures. Author Steve A. Anderson wished he had known about free collaborative library workshops rather than pay professionals; he would have "jumped at this resource!"

REFERENCES

ABC-CLIO. 2015. http://www.abc-clio.com/LibrariesUnlimited/ Authors/BecomeanAuthor.aspx.

Anderson, Steve A. 2015. E-mail communication and phone interview, December 15, 2015.

Archway Publishing. 2015. http://www.archwaypublishing.com. Accessed September 4, 2015.

Armenti, Peter. 2015. Library of Congress. Amateur Poetry Anthologies: A Guide to Finding Your Published Poems. November 9. https://www.loc.gov/rr/program/bib/contestpoems/. Accessed November 29, 2015.

Atlantic Monthly. 2015. "How Genius Works." http://www.theatlantic.com/special-report/how -genius-works. Accessed November 28, 2015.

Austin Public Library. 2015. http://www.austinlibrary.org/site/PageServer. Accessed September 4, 2015.

Book Launch Toolkit. 2015. http://authortoolkits.com/booklaunchtoolkit. Accessed September 4, 2015.

BookWorks. 2015. https://www.bookworks.com/. Accessed June 3, 2015.

Coker, Mark. 2014. "2015 Book Publishing Industry Predictions: Slow Growth Presents Challenges and Opportunities." *SmashwordsBlog.* http://blog.smashwords.com/2014/12/2015 -book-publishing-industry.html. Accessed December 31, 2015.

CreateSpace 2015. https://www.createspace.com. Accessed December 4, 2015.

Croan, Cody. 2015. Mid-Continent Public Library: Woodneath Press. http://www.mymcpl.org /about-us/woodneath-press. Accessed September 29, 2015.

E-mail Template for Newsletters. 2013. http://www.email-newsletter-template.com. Accessed November 29, 2015.

Fitzgerald, Jamie. 2013. "Notable Moments in Self-Publishing History: A Timeline." *Poets & Writers*, November/December. http://www.pw.org/content/notable_moments_in _selfpublishing_history_a_timeline.

Friedlander, Joel. 2015. "10 Things You Need to Know about Self-publishing." *The Book Designer*. http://www.thebookdesigner.com. Accessed July 26, 2015.

Google Slides. 2015. Create Beautiful Presentations. https://www.google.com/slides/about. Accessed November 29, 2015.

Gordon, Noah Eli. 2007. "Considering Chapbooks: A Brief History of the Little Book." *Jacket Magazine*, October. http://jacketmagazine.com/34/gordon-chapbooks.shtml. Accessed December 28, 2015.

Grant, Gavin. 2015. Small Beer Press. http://smallbeerpress.com. Accessed December 2, 2015.

Indy Publish. 2015. http://www.indypublish.com. Accessed September 4, 2015.

iUniverse. 2015. http://www.iuniverse.com. Accessed September 4, 2015.

Johnson County Public Libraries. 2014. *Elementia*. http://jocolibrary.org/teens/elementia. Accessed April 12, 2015.

Lightning Source. 2015. https://www.lightningsource.com. Accessed November 28, 2015.

Lossius, George. 2014. 5 Trends for Trade Publishing in 2014. http://publishingperspectives.com /2014/01/5-trends-for-trade-publishing-in-2014. Accessed December 31, 2015.

New Hanover County Public Library. 2015. http://libguides.nhclibrary.org/c.php?g=256048&p =1709558. Accessed November 28, 2015.

On Demand Books. 2015. Espresso Book Machine. http://ondemandbooks.com. Accessed September 4, 2015.

Phillips, Larry W., ed. 1984. *Ernest Hemingway on Writing*. New York: Scribner.

Real Life Poets. 2015. http://reallifepoets.org. Accessed September 4, 2015.

Scribd. 2015. https://www.scribd.com. Accessed November 28, 2015.

Seattle Arts and Lectures. 2015. Writers in the Schools. https://www.lectures.org/wits/writers_n _schools.php. Accessed June 18, 2015.

SELF-e Powered by Library Journal. 2015. http://self-e.libraryjournal.com. Accessed September 10.

Smashwords. 2015. https://www.smashwords.com. Accessed November 28, 2015.

Springfield City Library. 2015. http://www.springfieldlibrary.org/library/services/arts-entertainment -programs. Accessed November 28, 2015.

Staley, Lissa. 2015. "Leading Self-Publishing Efforts in Communities." *American Libraries* 46: 18–19.

Topeka Shawnee County Public Library. 2015. Community Novel Project. https://tscpl.org /community-novel/about. Accessed March 17, 2015.

Voell, Bryan. June 18, 2015. "Johnson County Library's Elementia: A Short History of Collaboration & Inspiration." *The Library as Incubator Project*. Accessed June 5, 2016.

Write Club. Hoover Public Library. 2015. http://www.hooverlibrary.org/services/write-club. Accessed September 4, 2015.

Write Life. 2015. http://thewritelife.com. Accessed June 3, 2015.

Writer's Digest. 2015. http://www.writersdigest.com. Accessed June 3, 2015.

Writer's Market. 2015. http://www.writersmarket.com. Accessed September 4, 2015.

Writer's Market 2016. 2015. Robert Lee Brewer, ed. Cincinnati, OH: Writer's Digest Books.

Appendix A

2012 COMMUNITY NOVEL PROJECT DETAILS

Based on assumptions about our reading community in 2012, we made a printable version of each week's chapter available for those who wanted to print out the work to share with others, in addition to publishing it online. Only a few years later this concession to serializing in multiple formats seems antiquated and unnecessary.

For the 2012 novel, we did design and layout in InDesign and used CreateSpace as our printer with distribution through Amazon.com. A surprising challenge we hadn't anticipated appeared in the final steps of the publishing process, as we discovered that the final price and delivery date couldn't be determined until the manuscript was approved for printing and the order for physical copies placed. Until then, we were estimating, hoping, and working quickly. We learned from this pilot project to build additional time into the delivery date and a financial buffer into the preorder price to lessen the stress of those unknowns.

Asking writers to create and edit fiction collaboratively while valuing each person's contributions was outside almost everyone's comfort zone initially. Lissa Staley recruited authors personally and individually, using a team-building approach, to play to people's strengths and work with their schedules, rather than arbitrarily assigning volunteers a week to write a chapter without fully engaging them in the project. The librarian project manager was required to wrangle 20 individual authors to each meet deadlines, as well as steer the course of the project toward the final collective goal.

An early author dropped out of the project and didn't complete the final draft of their chapter, even though the plot twist of the collaborative story was based on the major revelations in that chapter's contributions. The early draft of Chapter 5 was peer edited and published, but such setbacks threaten the integrity and the timeline of the project. Individual coaching was necessary to encourage authors to honor the chapters before their writing and leave space in the plot and character development for the authors and chapters to come. Some of this work would have been better divided between a dedicated continuity editor and the project manager.

If a library wants to consider the pace of the 2012 project for their undertaking, a glimpse at a week in the middle of that process is illuminating. Sample tasks from one week during simultaneous writing, editing, and serialization of 2012's *Capital City Capers*

During the week of June 4, 2012:

1. Chapter 10 author submits a draft to the library via e-mail. Library sends feedback. Chapter 10 author may choose to edit and send a final version the same week.
2. Library forwards the Chapter 10 first draft to the Chapter 11 writer to begin writing.
3. Chapter 7 is published on the library's Web site including the author picture and bio.
4. The recap section is updated to include Chapter 6.
5. Chapter 8 is copyedited for publication.
6. A reminder to the writer of Chapter 14, along with the copyright assignment form, request for photo and bio, and all of the existing chapters, summaries, and outline so they can prepare for their week to write.

Some of this work gathering information from writers could have been done at the outset of the project, if additional writers were not being recruited throughout the process. The pilot project relied on the early writers and readers to identify interested participants for the later chapters.

Appendix B

2013 COMMUNITY NOVEL PROJECT DETAILS

Speakeasy began with an organizational meeting, where 10 writers from our community met to discuss how the Community Novel Project could be improved in 2013, what roles people could fill to make the project a success, and what premise should be chosen for the group's novel. The premise for the story and the names of the main characters were established at that initial meeting, and *Speakeasy* was born. It would be a chick lit mystery with some history in which an anthropology grad student interviews a 108-year-old woman who doubts that all the adventures of her long life should be revisited.

Individual authors wrote the first few chapters but communicated closely with one another to create the characters and further develop the premise of the story. Because more authors took ownership of the original premise, it was almost inevitable that small factions would arise when the succeeding authors introduced major changes.

Participating authors chose which chapter they would like to write and were given an expected publishing date, but were told not to do too much prewriting, as each successive chapter follows the lead of the chapters published before, and there was no telling where the story could go. Even after experiencing the bombshell plot twist introduced by the author of Chapter 5 in *Capital City Capers*, we were unprepared for how thoroughly an agreed-upon premise could derail with the work of one chapter. In *Speakeasy*, the Chapter 7 author revealed that our grad student was actually an undercover police officer. This was a big surprise, not only for readers, but also for the author who was preparing to write Chapter 8.

A premise is not a script or a chapter-by-chapter outline, and individual authors will need to create a compelling plot. The guideline that we stress to all collaborative writers is that their chapter should build on the chapters that came before theirs, while leaving the story open to possibilities. Writers are encouraged to include bread crumbs and red herrings that future writers have the option to pick up and expand upon in their own chapters.

Authors who write for the second half of the novel have many more details to incorporate into a cohesive plotline. As with *Capital City Capers*, the final chapter of the novel was written in-house by library staff with input from other writers on the project and readers from the serialized story. For us, an important part of writing and publishing a community novel is having the story end on an upbeat note and reflect positively on our community.

In the author interviews, we asked writers to reflect on the writing process, including: why they participated, what they liked most about the premise, their first reaction after seeing the chapter before theirs, their favorite and least favorite addition from their own chapters, and what they hoped would or wouldn't happen in the chapters yet to come. Each author was also asked to contribute an author biography and photo to be included with online chapters and in the print edition of the book.

After a last minute line-by-line copyedit during print layout in the first year's project, we identified a need for additional peer editing earlier in the process. In order for library staff to focus on the management of the project, we needed to involve community participants in the editing process. We needed a way for everyone to edit the same document simultaneously, because we didn't want to burden anyone with reconciling suggested changes into one document. In early 2013, the freely available online collaborative tools were limited and not everyone had access to the same programs for word processing. The library's Web developer chose a free open source software called DokuWiki and installed it locally. A password on the Web server to the site prevented the public from reading the chapters early. We limited wiki editing access to a select group of editors by issuing individual logins, and encouraged participants to correct grammar, spelling, and punctuation errors. Editors were asked not to rewrite passages, but were encouraged to makes suggestions through editorial comments. Some collaborators also contacted the library project managers directly because they had feedback that they were not sure how to share constructively or appropriately on the shared wiki. While the project still needed a strong line-by-line edit at the conclusion, the peer editing throughout the process increased the quality of the serialized chapters and also gave the individual chapter authors some feedback on their work from their writing peers.

To serialize each chapter on the library Web site, we included a standard introduction to the project, then links to the chapter in several available formats for download, including PDF, EPUB, MOBI, mp3, and then the complete text of the chapter for reading online. At the time in 2013, taking the extra steps to convert the serialized chapters into files that were readable on the formats for dedicated e-readers like iPad, Nook, and Kindle seemed necessary to reach readers. We also created and linked to instructions for downloading and transferring the files to devices. We used the open source software Calibre to convert documents to EPUB and MOBI files. Calibre allowed us to add metadata including cover art, author, title, series information, publisher, publication date, and comments to the files.

To continue to model options for self-publishing formats, *Speakeasy* was made available as an audiobook. As downloadable audiobooks are popular with our library's readers, we believed that an audiobook format would make the story more accessible to our community. Our audiobook version was recorded into GarageBand on an iMac by a community volunteer. In keeping with the weekly chapter serialization, the weekly episodes were released through iTunes and were made available for download on the weekly blog post about the new chapter. The completed audiobook was released at the conclusion of the publishing process. At the time of the 2013 audiobook recording, the library only offered the necessary equipment for staff use.

The Topeka and Shawnee County Public Library added a digital makerspace for the public in 2015. Interested customers can now explore the hardware and software to record their own audiobook versions of their books. Whenever possible, we continue our commitment to modeling options that are freely available to the public, or made available through library resources. That said, the download statistics on the weekly audiobook did not justify continuing that serialized effort for future projects.

As the chapters were published and the novel project gained momentum and drew attention, authors promoted the project through local media. Publicity and marketing are components of self-publishing that are sometimes an afterthought to the process. We leveraged the library's media contacts to give participants authentic experiences in marketing this book. Several authors were interviewed for the *Topeka Capital-Journal* newspaper, and other authors recorded a podcast that was aired from the TSCPL Web site. As mentioned previously, authors shared their experiences as participants in the project through interviews. We encouraged authors to express personality in their answers, enabling writers to develop their voice and public persona. Anecdotally, several readers reported enjoying the interviews almost as much as reading the story.

Each week during serialization, the library's Web site published a new chapter and the author interview and shared the content through the library's Facebook and Twitter accounts. Readers and project writers shared and retweeted the story to their friends and followers. Using social media to reach potential readers with new chapters is a more active promotion technique than merely serializing on the library's Web site. We also discovered that readers were more inclined to share feedback about the book on social media sites than directly on the library Web site. Potential readers are more likely to discover new content when it is shared through personal contacts. Helping self-published writers practice these techniques on a project that is a community collaboration eases them into the graceful self-promotion that will be necessary for them to market their work.

Appearing at public events and conventions can be another way for self-published writers to reach readers. With *SpeakEasy*, several contributing writers promoted the finished book at the statewide Kansas Book Festival. At a library-sponsored booth, they could promote a book they helped create to receptive attendees of the festival. Like many aspects of the community novel project, providing structure and a supportive environment helps everyone try something new and learn from the process. For self-published writers, the ability to market oneself and one's work is crucial.

After the effort of completing the editing and print layout of the book, the preparation of the manuscript for Smashwords was straightforward. We followed the step-by-step instructions in the freely available "The Smashwords Style Guide" to remove much of the formatting we had so carefully added for the print version and create a clean manuscript that would display as expected on any e-reader (https://www.smashwords.com/about/how_to_publish _on_smashwords).

Since this is a library-published title, we hoped that readers could find the book alongside our library's e-book fiction options. Because the library is the creator of the community novel, we were allowed to add the e-book of *SpeakEasy* to our e-book collection through Overdrive. Restrictions for locally created content and loading individual titles vary by e-book platform. The e-book publishing industry is evolving quickly, and the services that libraries use to provide digital content to their customers are attempting to keep pace.

See our Web site: http://ebooks.tscpl.org/46CE9BFD-9318-4D84-9DF4-45ECE44C4E94 /10/50/en/ContentDetails.htm?id=964BE17C-1E7A-431E-A246-880E853FD89C.

Appendix C

2014 COMMUNITY NOVEL PROJECT DETAILS

SPIRITS OF OZ

One of the big gains of the 2013 project was increased collaboration that engaged writers in the creation of the novel from the beginning. In 2014 the project once again kicked off with an organizational meeting that invited the community of writers to share their premise ideas and agree on a direction for the book. At that meeting, writers received printed writing resources, discussed opportunities for project involvement, and agreed on a premise for each novel. The juvenile novel was established as the story of 12-year-old twins, Nico and Lola, whose parents were paranormal investigators and hosts of a struggling reality television show. The adventure begins when the spirits reach out to the kids instead of the adults for help with an otherworldly problem. Several chapters into the book, one of the contributing writers suggested the title *Spirits of Oz*. It was put to a vote and chosen unanimously.

Spirits of Oz aimed to raise the bar for participating writers in several ways. The novel was designed to be written by adults, but writers were encouraged to pair up with youth from the target audience to write in teams so that they would be co-writing with a young writer as well as collaborating on the book. One writer did pair up with a youth writer to collaborate on a chapter, and another writer engaged her children in the research and brainstorming for her chapter, but the remaining chapters were written by a single adult author. The young writer did serve as a beta reader for the remaining chapters, however, and offered feedback. Several writers remarked that it was beneficial to have the perspective of a reader from their target audience.

The novel was designed to be illustrated, which offered an opportunity for community artists to contribute their talents as well. This introduced new challenges, such as connecting with community artists, developing illustration guidelines, and scanning illustrations for publication. In this initial year of soliciting illustrations, we struggled to reach visual artists who were interested in contributing to the project. Our experiences in prior years of networking with aspiring writers did not transfer directly to aspiring artists in our community. Though we attempted to connect with artists at the local university and through local arts organizations, the opportunity we were offering did not seem to resonate with the experiences that local artists were seeking. It will be important moving forward to find ways to connect writers and illustrators, as many self-publishing authors are interested in increasing their knowledge of working with cover artists and using illustrations and graphic design to support their projects.

SUPERIMPOSED

The premise for the second novel of the 2014 Community Novel Project was creatively combined from several ideas suggested by community writers. In order to honor the interests of the writers contributing ideas while avoiding a premise that was too similar to the previous year, the group decided to use the narrative device of flashbacks. This allowed authors to choose between contributing chapters of historical fiction or contemporary fiction, and develop a mystery plot between the two timelines. We left the meeting with a novel setup—a wealthy, powerful man in Topeka is dying, and his lonely hospice worker wants to help him make peace with his past.

While the writers at the premise meeting agreed that mysteries would be revealed, as the authors developed the story, the surprising twists arrived more quickly than anyone could have anticipated. The writer who meticulously and poetically crafted the main character introduced in Chapter 2's flashback was shocked and dismayed by the plot twist in Chapter 6's flashback when her character is graphically killed and a new character loots his body and steals his identity. Writers with an interest in World War II added historically accurate details to their narrative, while other writers focused on character development. The plot twists in the present day were not any easier on the writers trying to continue the story. As the hospice worker character was sent to accomplish a task decidedly outside of her job description, the writers were challenged to continue her storyline throughout contemporary Europe. The twists make for a great story, and also reinforce for us as project organizers how difficult it can be to honor the contributions and expressed wishes of individual writers in a collaborative project.

Appendix D

2014—*SUPERIMPOSED* ACKNOWLEDGMENTS

Our writers go above and beyond for the Community Novel Project. This is evident in the acknowledgments pages of the published books. The following is adapted from the Acknowledgments section of *Superimposed*. We share this example to turn the abstract idea of collaborative fiction writing into something you can visualize. The complete acknowledgments more fully reflect the self-publishing process, but this excerpt focuses specifically on the contributions of the individual writers. The complete author interviews from all projects are available at http://tscpl.org/novel.

George Ismael Feliu Jr. and Stacy Spilker went first, and that is the hardest chapter of a community novel project. They took a premise, an inkling of an idea that had been agreed upon by the group, and created characters from almost nothing. Then they passed their chapter forward, turning complete control of those characters over to future writers. For George, we accidentally changed his character's name from Rimaldi to Grimaldi. It was an accident, but by the time we caught it, it was too late. Stacy's first flashback reads almost like poetry, giving us a taste of the past, but just not the past she thought she was creating.

In Chapter 3, Holly Mace laid out the basics of the fictional Holly's life. Her early details of the missing boyfriend and absent father were incorporated into the plot in more ways than she probably could have predicted. In Chapter 4, Brian W. Allen added historical adventure to our story. Dennis Smirl gave our project organizer a minor heart attack when he "went Game of Thrones" at the end of his chapter, introducing a major plot twist. Then, Diana Marsh took up where he left off and breathed life into the character who was left in the carnage.

In the first half of the present-day story, Rae Kary Staabs and her daughter Elizabeth Staab Van Deusen, Janet Jenkins Stotts, and A. M. Coffee introduced the many present-day characters that Joe Grimaldi can't trust. Painting a present-day scenario in which a wealthy man has no one he can rely on at the end of his life was crucial to the success of our story.

In Chapter 10, Elaine Greywalker used her flashback to explain a dying man's aversion to death, giving depth to both his past and his present and uniting the two parallel stories through her contribution to the novel.

Sarah Langley knows how to up the excitement level. The body count in her Chapter 11 may not be as high as in some of the earlier war scenes, but she takes the mysterious new character at the front door and quickly makes things happen for Holly.

Reoana Hemmingway worked flashback fictional magic in Chapter 12 to explain another identity twist—how the Salvatore Caló of the flashback chapter preceding hers became the Joe Grimaldi of Topeka, Kansas. As the plot twists continued, it became clear that the Joe Grimaldi of the present was hiding many mysteries.

In the second half of the book, first-time community novelists Mari White and Liv Howard threw themselves wholeheartedly into creating chapters that advanced an increasingly complex international story.

In Chapter 14, Annette Komma used her flashbacks to great advantage to connect the dots between characters. Her focus on the character of Peter changed the direction of the flashbacks and ultimately led toward our conclusion.

Crystal Green created a timeline for the novel and a list of unanswered questions that helped the authors after her and all of the editors look at the details raised throughout the story. With the extra work Crystal put into writing Chapter 16, writers were able to determine what red herrings could go unanswered and identify which of the most compelling parts of the plot should be included in the wrap-up of the storylines.

As appropriate for Chapter 17, late in the game for a 20-chapter outline, Steve Laird puts Holly under pressure to see if she will crack. His Pesha left some people rooting for a romance and some rooting for Holly to escape, and kept everyone reading to see what would happen next.

With Chapters 18 and 19, Nora E. Derrington and Craig Paschang came into this project near the conclusion and were given dozens of loose ends to wrap up in satisfying ways. Neither of them ran away from the challenge.

Marian Rakestraw hadn't even intended to contribute to this story, but as the project managers at the library were collaboratively writing chapter 20, she was working on the layout for the print novel. She was inspired and unexpectedly wrote the bank vault scene that appears at the conclusion of the story. We are quite glad she did. It's a great end to our novel and an excellent example of true collaborative writing.

Appendix E

2015 COMMUNITY NOVEL
PROJECT DETAILS

We started the 2015 project by posting reminders about the initial 2015 Community Novel Project event to local writer's groups on Facebook, distributing flyers at related library programs like the Local Author Workshop and the Great Writers, Right Here Author Fair, and e-mailing all previous participants. The initial event was also advertised in the Library News publication, which was mailed to all library cardholder households, as shown in the accompanying box.

Create the Community Novel

Saturday, January 31, 2015 | Noon–2 p.m. | Marvin Auditorium 101BC
    Learn self-publishing from start to finish with the library's Community Novel editorial team. You'll work with other writers to write, edit and publish a teen novel set in Topeka. Bring your premise ideas for a futuristic chooseable-path adventure.
    Learn more at tscpl.org/novel.

Handouts at the organizational meeting included an agenda to clearly define the goals of the session, guidelines to facilitate productive brainstorming along the established genre, and basic background explanation of the format of a chooseable-path story. We also had identified a need to address narrative point of view as a skill that writers could practice and improve, and provided handouts with guidelines. While a traditional Choose Your Own Adventure title is written in the second-person voice, we made the decision early on that the better skill development was in helping writers practice a close third-person point of view. Participant surveys encouraged writers to take a more active role in project management, writing, editing, illustrating, and online or print publishing.

After several years of premise meetings where we had vague goals, for 2015 we realized that training programs the library had implemented for meeting facilitation was very applicable in this setting working with community writers. The purpose of the session was for the group to reach consensus on a premise idea, setting, and character ideas. We established expected products and a timeline for progress and clearly communicated both in advance and on the agenda at the session. Lissa Staley utilized timers to maintain the pace of the work, flipcharts to capture and organize participant ideas, and a priority voting system to help guide participants toward consensus. When participants know what is expected of them, they are better able to deliver it. We succeeded in our fast-paced agenda because the group understood the scope of what we needed to accomplish. Some participants stepped up as peer-leaders to help others stay on task. The atmosphere was supportive, productive, and focused on the goal.

Agenda and Timeline

- 12:00–12:10 pm—Welcome, paperwork, and networking with other writers.
- 12:10 pm—Introductions and preview of communication tools for 2015 community novel.
- 12:20 pm—Vision for the project, actual deadlines calendar.
- 12:30 pm—Roles you could take in the project.
- 12:45—Establish premise: 10 minutes for pitching premises, 10 minutes to come to consensus, 10 minutes to develop premise idea together.
- 1:15 pm—Establish character(s) as informed by the premise decision. Is this a single character? Dual character? Ensemble cast?
- 1:45—Wrap-up, questions, and moving forward.

Another way we helped people focus was by establishing parameters for the community novel premise in advance. Reflecting on our past experience with collaborative premise development, we guided the group with criteria to focus the brainstorming process. A great story idea from an individual writer may look quite different from a workable concept for collaboration. In a group project, the emphasis is on creating a satisfying experience for writers and readers and the library. The focus at this point is on the process, rather than the product. We asked writers who wanted to share an idea to prepare a premise pitch of a few sentences, not a fully developed concept or outline.

Premise Guidelines

- Set in Topeka
- Set in "future"—can be near future
- Teen main characters
- PLOT-driven with lots of choices and many possible outcomes and twists
- Characters can remain consistent while ACTION drives story

As part of the premise meeting, we asked writers to consider how we would introduce the "future" Topeka in our book to quickly establish the setting for the readers. Suggestions for possible scenarios included terrorist attack, class wars, aliens, and natural disaster. Ultimately the group decided to set the book several generations in the future and use a time travel scenario.

At the conclusion of the premise meeting, the collaborators had established and agreed on the following:

- Title: *Time Harbor*
- High school students—they are part of the "elite" in the various schools throughout the city of Topeka
- They have applied to be part of a special program with the emphasis on history
- There will be two main characters born in 2033, one boy and one girl
- Location of time travel will be Forbes Field in 2050
- Limits will be set in Section 1 that will help to establish focus for the book
- The adventures will (for the most part) occur in the past
- Parents born between 2000 and 2003
- Grandparents born between 1970 and 1975
- Great-grandparents born between 1940 and 1950
- Character cheat sheet advised
- Syllabus could show what is supposed to happen so that it's more obvious when things start to go wrong
- Parents will sign a waiver to participation in the activity as a "safe, transformational experience"

The group raised the following questions but did not answer them: What will the future be like? And how will it affect the plot and characters without being distracting?

Coming out of the premise meeting with a dozen collaborators agreeing to these details about the story set us up for a successful project. In fact, instead of one author taking on Chapter 1, the collaborating authors self-selected to work together to further develop the writing and documents that would set up the character paths. Because the individual chapters would be written in close third-person point of view and follow different characters on their adventures, the newspaper article, handout, safety guide, and other ephemera presented before the first character paths established the futuristic world and time travel scenario for readers.

Community Novel Project: Character Workshop

Thursday, February 26, 2015 • 6:30–8:30 p.m.
Marvin Auditorium 101C

Fine-tune your fiction writing techniques. Compare narrator perspectives and points of view. Learn how to build character backstory using continuity notes, photos, and worksheets. Discuss how to give your character a unique voice and maintain character integrity throughout a novel. tscpl.org/novel.

For our second writing program of the year, we focused on character development using the characters of *Time Harbor* as examples while we discussed broader techniques that would be helpful for any fiction writer. Our plans included overview of project, current premise, reviewing character worksheets, an interactive exercise about creating a character, meeting our two characters, discussing chooseable-path plot structure, and looking ahead for the month before publication. Handouts included freely available online articles on accidental point of view changes, authorial intrusion, stepping out of character, character profiles, and writing voice.

The deliberate planning and collaborative development of *Time Harbor* was a departure from previous community novel projects, which rushed to get a writer started on Chapter 1 with minimal structure. With the setup of the premise established and the character profiles created through the group's efforts, the story paths for each character could finally begin.

So how does one plot a multiple-path, multiple-character adventure story, written by different authors simultaneously? Contributing writer Craig Paschang made a careful study of similar novels and shared his thoughts with the group. He wrote in an email to the authors in December 2015:

> You can't have a traditional three act play plot structure in a chooseable path adventure, but you can still be challenged in different ways. If you choose paths that move your character through ways that would likely force them to grow (like in a traditional plot) then you advance. And if you choose the more silly or limiting plot choices, you get the less satisfying endings. If you make it farther down the tree, the endings are happier.

Having three writers writing simultaneously on three separate character paths, each of which diverged into two more paths per character, each with a new writer, could have been very confusing. Fortunately, Craig Paschang developed a plot diagram, which project managers used to direct writers on their specific paths. Writers did not read what was happening on other paths until they were done writing because trying to understand all of the possible paths at the same time likely would have led to frustration. Writers were encouraged to include action and adventure in their section that would advance the plot, but to avoid character development that would be outside of the established character profiles.

As always with our community novel project and collaborative writing, we encouraged writers to be considerate of those who would be continuing the story. One benefit of a chooseable-path novel is the necessity of multiple endings, which gave authors the option to write a creative conclusion. Some writers used that opportunity of writing an ending to explore huge plot twists, tragedy, and romance without having to consider the repercussions on the overall story.

The group originally agreed that the reader could choose to follow either the main boy or main girl character's storyline, but a history teacher was added to the mix in the prologue. The genre of the novel was established as young adult fiction and so the central characters that the reader should anticipate succeeding are teenagers. The history teacher is revealed to be somewhat nefarious in the prologue document "Video Diary of Clark J. Detrick, Educator and Eminent Time Traveler," and while readers can follow his story paths to several historical destinations, the paths quickly lead to his demise in both 1866 at the construction of the Kansas State Capitol building and the 1937 shootout at the downtown post office between FBI agents and bank robbers.

No happy endings are written for this adult character who is presumed to cause the time travel mechanism to malfunction. The two teenagers, Han and Mai, each have multiple solitary paths through the past, with many disappointing or unfulfilling endings. Mai time travels to the summer of 1951, notable in local history for the first trial of the groundbreaking *Brown vs. Board of Education* decision and a significant Kansas River flood, and then travels to the 1988 grand opening of our current regional shopping mall. Han time travels to the day of the 1966 tornado that destroyed a path through the city of Topeka and then back to 1901 during Carrie Nation's visit to the capital city.

They each have a single ending in which one of them returns to the present but the other is lost. Only one possible path for each of them leads to the satisfying conclusion of the novel in which not only are both students returned safely to 2050, but the entire city is revealed to have played a part in their rescue. As in previous years, this final happy ending was written by library staff in collaboration with other project writers.

Community Novel Project: Book Layout Workshop

Tuesday, June 23, 2015 • 6:30–8:30 p.m.

Marvin Auditorium 101C

Learn self-publishing from start to finish with the library's Community Novel editorial team. Share tips for consistent editing and style, and use Microsoft Word templates from CreateSpace's self-publishing platform to edit and design a print-ready manuscript. Get hands on with tscpl.org/novel.

In previous years the participants who helped with the novel's print layout design met with library staff individually to learn how to use CreateSpace to prepare this project for publication. To meet community demand for information on this topic, we advertised a presentation that covered the terminology of book layout and detailed the steps to consider when self-publishing a book. Using screenshots from previous community novel projects, we shared examples of setup, templates, timelines, required formatting checks, ordering, pricing, and shipping.

The library program was based on CreateSpace because it was the tool used in our project, and it provides blank Word templates in the correct size for various cover dimensions. We have used Smashwords for e-publishing after the print layout manuscript is complete. We pointed out that other platforms for printing books are available and discussed e-book and print-on-demand possibilities. Our project continues a commitment to using self-publishing tools that are freely available on public computers, and because CreateSpace and Smashwords both provide step-by-step guides for their products, library support on how to use these tools is minimal.

Participants contributed their experiences with e-book and print publication options in a facilitated discussion that revealed the many factors involved in any self-publisher's decision-making process. The results revealed a wide spectrum of challenges, from the huge stack of books forever stockpiled in the garage to the virtual book signing for the e-book-only edition.

REFERENCE

Paschang, Craig. 2015. E-mail message to the author, December 16.

Appendix F

AUTHORS WORKSHOP AND AUTHOR FAIR

Our library transitioned from monthly Sunday Afternoons with a Kansas Author to an annual author fair and an annual writer's workshop. Over the past three years, we have improved our events based on participant feedback. While libraries and communities vary, what we learned and changed should help libraries interested in offering similar programming.

In 2013, the first year of the programming change, a two-part event included a novice writer's forum preceding the afternoon author fair event. The forum included a panel of four successful authors formed to give advice and encouragement to all of the participating authors. The author fair offered all authors who applied an opportunity to market and sell their published works to the community. The library advertised the Local Author Fair to the community as a library event and allowed authors to handle their own sales directly to browsing customers. The forum was marketed only to the authors who applied, as a benefit for participating as a vendor in the fair.

The demand for the forum was so great and the feedback was so positive that the library decided to repeat both events the following year but to split them into distinct events.

By attending the local author forum a few months in advance of the fair, authors could get advice they could use at the fair in December. This also allowed the library to advertise the author fair to aspiring writers in the community who attended the first local writer's workshop. The separate events Local Writer's Workshop and Great Writers, Right Here were created.

LOCAL WRITER'S WORKSHOP

The Local Writer's Workshop is a morning of TED-style talks delivered by successful regional authors. We learned that the people interested in attending the Local Writer's Workshop to increase their skills were a different audience than the authors who were ready to market their published work at the fair. For two years, we have focused on providing insight and advice for aspiring authors who aim to publish their work. The workshop topics go beyond fiction writing and span all aspects of the craft, as well as publishing and marketing for non-fiction, memoir, poetry, fiction, and graphic novels.

The workshop opens with an inspiring keynote speaker and then narrows into specific topics. In 2015, Angela Cervantes's "How a Bookworm Became a Children's Author" showcased her path to publication including rejections, rewrites, and the challenges of writing a second book under contract. "The Writer/Artist Collaboration" illuminated Ande Parks's behind-the-scenes process of working with an artist to create the graphic novel *Capote in Kansas*. Self-published author Brian W. Allen revealed niche marketing techniques in "Ten Things to Sell a Thousand Books." Topeka poet Israel Wasserstein addressed the nuts and bolts of submissions and building a writing resume within and outside academia in "The Business of Being a Writer." In "Research for Writers," James L. Young encouraged writers to include crucial historical details in a believable narrative, speaking from his experience as a doctoral student in history as well as a novelist of alternative history. Leah Sewell, founder of the Topeka Writer's Workshop, shared advice from her experience and a call to action on how to effectively run or participate in a writer's group in "Build Your Writing Community."

While the topics and speakers in previous and future years are intentionally varied, the theme of the event is practical advice and encouragement to persist in pursuing a writing life. We identify speakers based on their strengths. While they develop their own talk, we specify a topic and work with them to create a program description to advertise the event. In intentionally creating a diverse lineup, we appeal to a wider audience of aspiring and established writers. No one is forced into sharing competing success stories; each speaker is an expert on his or her topic.

LOCAL AUTHOR FAIR

Much like the Community Novel Project, we have experimented and improved the Great Writers, Right Here author fair each year.

The first year, we accepted paper applications from nearly 90 authors, even accepting new applicants a few days before the event. Our overriding goal was to offer an opportunity for every interested author to participate as a vendor and sell his or her work. In the second year, we streamlined the process by creating an online application form. We required authors to submit a brief biography and head shot, as well as cover images and blurbs for books that they wished to sell, which provided our team with the information we needed to successfully market the event to our community. For some emerging authors, this provided an opportunity to engage in the marketing process. Our team provided feedback for some applicants that enabled them to raise the quality of their marketing materials. This year, our team also reached out directly to some of the most successful published writers in our community to invite them to headline the event and draw in more customers. We place emerging authors side-by-side with established authors, sorting by book genre, not author status. Customers may be drawn in by familiar names and titles, but they'll also have an opportunity to discover other regional authors.

Feedback from first-year participants overwhelmingly indicated that the event was too crowded; the following year we spread authors throughout the library, placing some vendor tables in high-traffic hallways rather than in the auditorium where the main event was held. This experiment failed because the authors outside the auditorium felt separated from the action and reported poor sales.

In the third year, we were committed to keeping all authors together in the same room. We couldn't make the room bigger, so we had to accept fewer authors. Our criteria for acceptance included local appeal, quality of marketing materials, and timely and complete application. These criteria allowed us to curate a public event that showcased our region's literary talent. In order to make the event more enjoyable for attendees, we also included readings from six featured authors, which took place in the same room as the event. Seating was provided for those who wanted to devote their attention to the readings, but the sound system allowed customers to hear readers from anywhere in the auditorium as they continued to browse.

Each year we aim to host a fantastic event for our reading public, while also providing an opportunity for authors to network with one another, grow professionally, sell books, and reach new readers.

INDEX

ABOUT THE AUTHORS

ROBERT J. (BOB) GROVER is a retired university administrator and professor emeritus of library and information management at Emporia (Kansas) State University. He previously taught at University of South Florida and University of Southern California. He has authored numerous refereed journal articles and book chapters, and he has co-authored *Assessing Information Needs: Managing Transformative Information Services*; *Helping Those Experiencing Loss: A Guide to Grieving Resources*; *Introduction to the Library and Information Professions*; and *Evolving Global Information Infrastructure and Information Transfer*, all published by Libraries Unlimited.

CARMAINE TERNES has been involved in secondary education for more than 30 years as an English teacher and school librarian. A member of ALA, AASL, Kansas Library Association, Kansas Association of School Librarians, and YALSA, Carmaine presents at state and local conferences and has contributed to professional journals. She sponsors the Emporia High School Creative Writing Club and Future Educators of America and has been active in the Young Writers' Conference and the Kansas Learning First Alliance. She has served as President of the Kansas Association of School Librarians, is a member of the Emporia State University Summer Institute for School Librarians planning committee, and an AASL Learning4Life state coordinator. Colleagues have recognized her with the Emporia Public Library Super Friend of the Year in 2009 and the Hopkins Foundation Education Award in 2014. Carmaine is passionate about learning and providing services to benefit students.

LISSA STALEY is a public services librarian at Topeka and Shawnee County Public Library, Topeka, Kansas. She is the project organizer of four collaboratively written and published novels and since 2004 has developed programming that supports skill building for writers. She is the Topeka Municipal Liaison with National Novel Writing Month. She focuses on constantly improving customer experience and freely sharing successful ideas with other librarians.

MIRANDA ERICSSON is a public service specialist at the Topeka and Shawnee County Public Library (TSCPL) in Topeka, Kansas. She has a passion for regional writing, and she represented the library as a member of the 2015 Kansas Notable Books Committee and 2015 Poet Laureate of Kansas Selection Committee. You'll find her profiles of Kansas writers paired with original interviews on TSCPL's Books Blog. Miranda creates library programs and events that support Topeka's writing community. Current projects include the Community Novel Project, NaNoWriMo, Local Writers Workshop, and Great Writers, Right Here author fair.

KELLY VISNAK, PhD, is associate university librarian for scholarly communications with the University of Texas at Arlington. The University Libraries extend instruction and collections beyond traditional programming to create scholarship services that are openly available to the wider academic community and the general public. This includes the dynamic FabLab, Academic Plaza, audio booth and digital repositories that are pushing the edge for publishing research, and learning innovations with the "makerspaces" and "open" movements.